legend into language

Moira Andrew

Acknowledgements

The author, editor and publishers would like to give special thanks to the staff of Abertillery Primary School, Gwent; Dinas Powys Infants School, Vale of Glamorgan; and Malpas Church Junior School, Newport, for their generous help and support during the making of *Legend into Language*. They would also like to thank the children of these schools for their enthusiastic co-operation and for their many contributions of art and language work.

Night

Night is a deep forest,
snagging dreamtime on its
outstretched branches.

Night fixes me with its
evil eye, snarls my feet
in dark tangled roots.

Moonlight scribbles
across shadows, highlights
my sense of loneliness.

Like the last person left
on earth, I stumble from tree
to bone-bare tree.

Dreams lure me on to
dangerous pathways, tempt
me to sightlessness.

I tell beads of blackness;
sloe, raven, jet, ebony.
Bat-dark depths entice me.

I hear the moon-songs of
dying leaves, the night cry
of mosses, stars sighing.

Moira Andrew

First published in 1998 by BELAIR PUBLICATIONS LIMITED
Albert House, Apex Business Centre, Boscombe Road, Dunstable, LU5 4RL, United Kingdom.

© 1998 Moira Andrew
Reprinted 1999.

Series editor: Robyn Gordon   Design: Lynn Hooker
Photography: Kelvin Freeman   Line drawings: Andrea Heath

Printed in Hong Kong through World Print Limited

ISBN: 0 94788 269-3

Contents

	PAGE
Introduction	4
AFRICA "The Enchanted Gourd"	5
AUSTRALIA "The Rainbow Serpent"	12
CHINA "The Willow Pattern Story"	19
ENGLAND "St George and the Dragon"	27
GREECE "Flight to the Sun"	35
INDIA "The Great Storm"	42
NORTH AMERICA "The Night Moon-Woman was Angry"	49
SCOTLAND "The Seal-Wife"	57
WALES "The Magic Harp"	65

INTRODUCTION

Myths and legends are stories from long ago. Such stories can increase our understanding of the past. Few were written down. Most were handed on from grandparent to grandchild, or from one storyteller to another. They often try to explain things which, in these modern days, would probably have a scientific explanation. Sometimes they are known as 'creation myths', told as a way of coming to terms with how the world might have been formed. Often, too, these stories have a religious significance.

Myths and legends are usually interesting and colourful stories, with the breath of life lived in a different time and place and are therefore an ideal starting-point for creative work, both in language and art. Working from a range of resources, I have retold the legends in this book using my own voice and the language of today.

It is hoped that the teachers and children who use this book will find their own new ways of expressing the experience of legend in a variety of follow-up ideas in artwork and writing.

Moira Andrew

Manu's magic garden – see page 47

A STORY FROM AFRICA
The Enchanted Gourd

Chipo was an African boy who loved listening to his grandfather's stories. His favourite was the tale of an enchanted gourd. 'Whoever owns this gourd,' said grandfather, 'will never again need to hunt or fish, never need to plant seeds or cut the corn! It is filled with an everlasting store of food.'

'Has anyone ever found the enchanted gourd, grandfather?' asked Chipo. 'No, nor ever likely to,' said grandfather. 'It is guarded by the Witch of the Great Waters. She is as fierce as a jackal. She will never give it up!'

When Chipo grew to be a young man, there was a great drought in the land. The corn withered, the animals died and still the rains did not come. Everyone in the village became like a bag of bones. 'The Enchanted Gourd could save my people,' Chipo said.

So next morning he set off to find it. 'Help everyone as you go along, my boy,' said grandfather. 'But take care, the Witch of the Great Waters is very dangerous.' Chipo met some men cutting grass and stopped to help them. 'Please, can you tell me where the Witch of the Great Waters lives?' he asked. The grass-cutters showed him the path to take.

He walked on until he came to a group of herdsmen and stopped to help them herd their cows. They told him to walk on until he came to the cool blue waters of the river. There he saw some young girls carrying jars of water on their heads. For a time Chipo helped them with their work too. Then the water-carriers showed him a line of hills in the distance. 'Go across the hills,' they said. 'You will come to a deep black lake. The Witch of the Great Waters lives there, so take care.'

Chipo was tired, but he trudged across the hills until he came to the lake. By this time it was night and the lake looked deep and dark and dangerous in the moonlight. 'Witch of the Great Waters,' called Chipo. 'Please may we borrow the enchanted gourd? We have no food and my people are dying!'

There was a great noise, like a thunderous waterfall, and the most fearsome-looking creature rose dripping from the depths of the lake. She was covered in mud and slime. 'Who calls my name?' she thundered. 'It is I, Chipo,' said Chipo in a small voice. The witch reached down and lifted him like a stick insect between her fingers. 'You will make a tasty snack,' she boomed. Still holding Chipo tight, she swam down to the bottom of the lake. Chipo shut his eyes and held his breath.

Soon he found himself in a cave under the deep waters. The witch put him in a dark corner and forgot about him. She was much too hungry! Chipo watched as the giantess rolled a great yellow gourd across the floor. She tapped it once, twice, three times, and the gourd split open. Yams and mangoes and mealie-corn spilled across the floor. 'The Enchanted Gourd!' Chipo said to himself.

The witch gobbled up all the food she could manage. Then she slumped to the floor, fast asleep, snoring like a great whale. This was Chipo's chance. Quietly he rolled the gourd out of the cave. Then he clung on tight as it bobbed up to the top of the Great Waters.

Soon Chipo was rolling across the hills, riding the enchanted gourd like a great yellow tiger. Then the witch woke up. She was so angry that thunder echoed among the clouds and lightning streaked across the sky. 'Stop thief!' she roared.

Just as Chipo felt the breath of the witch on his neck, he saw the water-carriers. 'Help!' he called. The girls emptied water from their jars and it became a torrent, tumbling the witch off her feet.

'Thank you,' said Chipo, rolling the gourd along the path with great speed. But the witch was catching up. Then Chipo saw the herdsmen. 'Help!' he called, and at once the herdsmen changed their cows into raging bulls and they chased the witch away.

Chipo and the gourd rolled on, but again the witch almost caught them. By this time Chipo was very tired. When he met the grass-cutters still scything the grass, he could only whisper 'Help!' The grass-cutters swirled up great tornadoes of pollen and that made the witch sneeze and sneeze! She sneezed so much that she blew Chipo and the gourd all the way back to the village where grandfather and the villagers were waiting.

Chipo tapped the gourd once, twice, three times, and it split open, spilling fruit and fish, corn and spices all across the ground. 'Eat up,' said Chipo. 'From now on, everyone can have as much food as they want and nobody need ever starve!'

5

SPEAKING AND LISTENING

Listening

- Listen to the story of 'The Enchanted Gourd' read aloud. In groups, choose poems about Africa and read them to find out what they tell about life there - climate, homes, clothes, food, and so on. (For example, 'Drought' by Accabre Huntley, 'Look' and 'Have a mango' by Grace Nichols.) Contrast and compare what you have learned from the poems with the view of African life suggested in the legend of 'The Enchanted Gourd'.

- 'When we were very young': Chipo *loved listening to his grandfather telling stories.* Older people often have very interesting stories to tell about things that happened when they were children. Ask around to see if grandparents might be willing to come into school to share stories about their childhood. Listen to their stories with great courtesy and make up ten questions to help them remember details which might be of great interest to today's children.

Drought

- It says in the story that once *'there was a great drought in the land'.* Discuss what this means and talk about what happens in fields and gardens in a drought. In many countries famine follows drought. Discuss why this is so. Think about the problems and difficulties - and tragedies - which famine can cause, especially among children. Find out what some of the charities do to help the children of countries where famine has struck.

Everlasting food

- The story tells us that the owner of the enchanted gourd *'will never again need to hunt or fish, never need to plant seeds or cut the corn!'* Discuss this idea. Most of us don't do any of these things, so how do we provide food for our families instead?

- Discuss what you would like to see spilling out of the enchanted gourd if it came into your possession. What kinds of food would you want? Who would you share with? Try to encourage the children to think more carefully about healthy eating, variety in food, and sharing food with others.

LANGUAGE ACTIVITIES

Drought

- Talk about what drought means in our own towns and villages, then discuss the consequences in countries like Africa. List six things that you would miss in a period of drought, for example, flowers, green grass, cool fresh rain. Use this list as the basis for a poem about drought, beginning some of your lines with the word 'no', then contrasting these ideas with what a drought-stricken garden or street looks like.

Your poem might look like this:

> *No rain, no puddles,*
> *no fresh wet smell of grass,*
> *no green, no breeze,*
> *just the hot yellow eye*
> *of the sun glaring*
> *from a cloudless sky.*

Recipe book

- Ask parents, governors, teachers, dinner ladies and friends of the school for a favourite recipe. Organise the recipes into sections, for example, *Cakes and biscuits, Vegetarian, Sweets and desserts,* etc. Using a mixture of best writing and word-processing, copy out the recipes one to a page. (Make sure that spelling is accurate and that measures are correct.)

  Add a commentary about each, if possible. For example, you might find that one recipe is an old family favourite so that you can add the donor's first memory of eating it. Should another recipe have a regional flavour, write two or three sentences about where it originated. Try to make the book as interesting and individual as possible. Using a black pen (so that the pages can be photocopied), make a frame for each recipe. The frames should reflect the ingredients needed.

  The books can be copied and collated at the local teachers' resource centre. Put the books on display, selling them to help towards your chosen famine charity fund.

The enchanted fridge

- Write an up-to-date version of 'The Enchanted Gourd', taking it into your own time and place. Instead of Chipo, make your hero/heroine someone you might meet in school. Rewrite the adventure, following the structure of the original story but, for example, making the grass-cutters into traffic wardens, the water-carriers into dinner ladies, the herdsmen into house or road-builders, etc.

- Replace the gourd with a fridge or freezer. Make up a science-fiction character to take the place of the Witch of the Great Waters, and give him/her a suitable place in which to live. Make a book for the story and illustrate it as you go along.

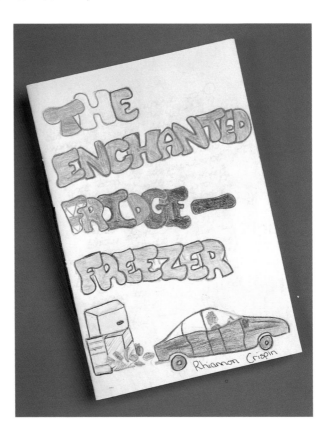

A tasty snack

- *The witch lifted Chipo like a stick insect between her fingers.* Can you think of any more stories where giants meet very little people? (You might suggest *Mrs Pepperpot, Tom Thumb* or *Gulliver's Travels.*)

- Imagine that you have been turned into a very small person. It would be difficult to do things which are usually very easy, for example, getting out of bed, turning on the tap, looking out of the window. Everyone else would be the size of a giant. Imagine meeting the family cat!

- Write a page of your diary in which you are very small indeed, like Chipo in the witch's fingers, and that a giant has just spied you as a tasty snack! Write about your escape and the adventures you have before getting back to normal on the stroke of midnight.

'When we were very young'

- Listen to the stories told by older people. (See *Speaking and listening*.) Make notes on what you can remember and ask questions to fill in on anything you don't understand, or where you need to know more. You might like to use a tape recorder to help you remember everything.

- Using the notes, choose a story to write in an autobiographical style, as though you are the child you have been hearing about. Try to ensure that everyone chooses a different topic. Make the stories and descriptions of what life was like for the grandparents when they were young into a class scrapbook. Vary the content of the scrapbook as much as possible. Some stories might be written as poems, as letters, as diary entries or as straight pieces of descriptive prose. Add photographs (or copies), cuttings from old newspapers and illustrations of clothes, household items, and so on.

The Great Waters

- When Chipo reached the Great Waters, it was night and the lake looked '*deep and dark and dangerous in the moonlight*'. Imagine how the water would shine, the shadows made by the clouds, the sounds of night.

Write a short poem (five to seven lines only) to describe a lake or the sea by moonlight.

> *Moonlight on the water*
>
> *The lake shines like a mirror,*
> *shadows sailing on glass.*
> *Mountains stand guard,*
> *silhouetted, sinister.*
> *The night is alive with wings*
> *swooping and diving like ghosts.*

Make the poem a simple descriptive piece, suggesting mood and movement and colour - or lack of it.

CUT OUT WINDOW

CLEAR PLASTIC

EDGE THE LAKE IN SILVER PEN

SILVER

Write a play

- 'The Enchanted Gourd' has a number of different characters and will make an ideal play. Read or listen to the story again, then work out how many main characters are needed: Chipo, grandfather and the witch. (You might also include the gourd and give it some lines to say!) You will need grass-cutters, herdsmen, water-carriers, villagers and children - as many or as few as you like.

Some of the words are already set out in the story, others you will need to make up. To work on the dialogue, think what you would say as the tale moves along. Think first of how grandfather would gather all the children of the village around him, sitting cross-legged round a flickering fire. Then he would begin his story...and so on to the end.

- Mix the story words with made-up dialogue. You can add as much detail as you like, or change the stories as you go along. Think about the way stories you have read in books are adapted for television. They are often quite different!

- When your play is finished, choose your characters and give out scripts. Don't worry if the actors change your lines as they work. This happens! When you are ready, ask children from another class to be your audience.

ART ACTIVITIES
The enchanted gourd
- Make a gourd in papier mâché. When it is dry and decorated, you can split it open at the top and have a variety of fruit and vegetables spilling out - all in paper mâché. Gourds are not easy to come by, so use a football or a balloon, as a base. Use real fruit and vegetables for the rest.

To make papier mâché, you will need:
> lots of old newspaper, torn into strips
> small packet of wallpaper paste made up according to the manufacturer's instructions

You will also need:
> base shape (e.g. balloon, fruit, vegetables)
> petroleum jelly
> white emulsion paint
> acrylic or poster paints
> polyurethane varnish (best in spray form)

This is what you do:
> Tear the newspaper into strips or small pieces and make up the paste in a tray. Use a paintbrush to cover lots of pieces at once.
> Cover the base shape with a thin layer of petroleum jelly.
> Smooth overlapping pieces of pasted paper on to the base.
> You will need several layers. Leave to dry thoroughly. (This might take two or more days.)
> Cut the shape open with a craft knife (adult help needed), and ease the paper shape away from the fruit. Then paste more paper strips over the join and leave to dry once more. (If using a balloon shape for the gourd, you can simply leave this inside.)
> Prime the shape by painting with white emulsion.
> Use bright acrylics to paint the surface - either in realistic colours (for example, reds, greens and yellows for peppers) or invent fantastic fruit (blue lemons, perhaps) and, when dry, decorate with patterns.
> Leave to dry, and then varnish. **(See photograph.)**

WANTED! posters

- Paint a large portrait of the witch. To make her look fearsome, think about the shape and colour of her face. Give her unusual spiky hair, spots, monster eyes and teeth, perhaps. Print the word WANTED! in large letters at the top of your poster. If you wish, add a paragraph of written description.

A collection of poems

- Make a class collection of African poems, mixing those you have written (see *Language activities*) with those you have found (see *Speaking and listening*). Write each poem out in "best", taking care to design the page as a whole. Make an appropriate frame, for example, leaves and fruit, water and waves, sunshine with the first few drops of rain, etc., or illustrate in felt-tip pen.

- For the cover, make a design of fruit and vegetable prints. Use a heavy paper. Cut the fruit and vegetables in half (lemons, onions and peppers make interesting shapes), and dip into fairly thick poster paint. Carefully press the fruit-shape on to the backing paper, using one colour of paint at a time. When each is dry, overlap with another shape in a different colour.

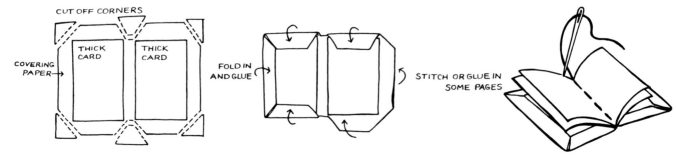

Spoon puppets

- 'The Enchanted Gourd' can be made into a simple puppet play for use with the youngest children (see *Language activities*). Make all the characters in the same way, using wooden spoons. Draw a face on the back of the spoon, using felt-tip pens. Tape on hair made from scraps of knitting wool. For the clothes, cut scraps of cloth about 40cm wide and long enough to cover the spoon handle. Wrap the cloth round the spoon and fasten with an elastic band.

DRAW ON FACE IN FELT TIP PEN

TIE SHORT LENGTHS OF WOOL TOGETHER FOR HAIR

40cm

FABRIC

ELASTIC BAND

USE A SMALLER SPOON AND BRIGHT PATTERNED FABRIC TO MAKE CHIPO

USE PLAIN WHITE FABRIC FOR THE WITCH – SPLASH ON BROWN PAINT FOR MUD AND GREEN FOR SLIME

GRANDFATHER HAS COTTON WOOL HAIR AND BEARD

- Design a spoon for each character, remembering to give grandfather a cotton wool beard and a brown patched cloak. Use a big spoon for the witch and give her coloured hair and a spotty face. Use a variety of materials so that each character looks different. Use a painted ball as the gourd.

- To perform the play, let the children hide just below a table-top, holding the spoons by the handle beneath the 'cloaks'. Have a narrator and let the performers say the words of each character as their part comes along in the story.

Chipo's adventure

- Using a large sheet of paper, outline the path that Chipo took on his way to meet the Witch of the Great Waters, starting from the village. Show the huts, the parched fields, the sun. Show the grass-cutters among tall grasses, the herdsmen and their cows, the water-carriers by *'the cool blue waters of the river'*. Next have a mountain range and the deep dark lake with the witch rearing out of the waters with a great splash.

Deep, dark and dangerous

- The lake was *'deep and dark and dangerous in the moonlight'*. To make a picture of the lake at night, cut out a large irregular shape in mid-blue paper. Overlay this with pools of moonlight (silver paper), dark depths (shiny dark blue/purple/black papers) and cover the whole with clingfilm or OHP acetate.

- On a dark background, paint brooding mountains, trees in silhouette, and paste the 'lake' in position. Add a cut-out silver moon and give the entire picture a sense of magic and mystery. (See *Language activities*.)

A STORY FROM AUSTRALIA
The Rainbow Serpent

Once, long ago in Dreamtime when the world was new, Chinimin quarrelled with his father, the spirit god who had made everything in earth and heaven. Never before had anyone dared disagree with him, so he was furious.

'You will suffer for this, Chinimin! Mark my words!' he shouted.

Chinimin ran like the wind, over rocks and stones until he came to the wild roaring river. He tried to swim across the river to escape from the spirit world to the earth. But his father saw what was happening and sent a swarm of bees to stop him. The bees buzzed and hummed and swarmed in a great black cloud. They stung Chinimin's face and neck. They stung his hands and feet. Chinimin was in such pain that he rushed back from the wild roaring river into the spirit world where his father was waiting. The old spirit god yelled, 'I'm going to teach you a lesson, boy, a lesson you will never forget!' and he raised a huge knobbly club and brought it down on Chinimin's head. Chinimin felt quite dizzy, but he managed to draw a spear from his belt.

All along the bank of the wild roaring river Chinimin and his father battled day and night. It was a battle to the death.

As the sun rose in the morning sky, Chinimin thrust the spear into his father's side and the old spirit god doubled up with pain. He tumbled into the wild roaring river, almost mortally wounded, twisting and writhing in agony, like a great serpent.

Until then, the earth had been parched and dry, but the waters of the river rose as the spirit god splashed and squirmed like a serpent. Still writhing in pain, he left the spirit world and landed on the earth. His body made huge craters in the ground. Water from the river swirled behind him, filling the hollows to make lakes and rivers and streams.

As water from the spirit river soaked into the earth, plants of every colour appeared like a great patchwork quilt thrown across the land. Red flowers sprang from the serpent god's blood, blue from the waters of the river and golden yellow from the rays of the sun where the serpent god had torn a hole in the sky.

Chinimin stood on the other side of the spirit world and wondered at what he had done. 'I'm sorry, father,' he called. 'Will you come back across the wild roaring river?' But the serpent god was still in pain and still very angry with his son. 'Go away!' he shouted. 'You are no longer fit to be my son! I'll show you how angry I am!'

He sent for the darkest clouds and the strongest winds to create a ferocious storm. Clouds crashed and thunder roared. Lightning flashed and fierce rain lashed the land. This went on for seven days and seven nights. The flowers bent their heads, the trees swayed and the grass was hammered flat on the ground. Chinimin watched from the banks of the wild roaring river. 'Stop, father,' he called. 'You will ruin the beautiful world that you are making!'

But even the great serpent god was beginning to tire. The wind grew gentle, the rain slowed and a pale yellow sun appeared in the sky. The flowers stood straight and tall, more beautiful than ever. The trees stretched out their leaves and the grasses sang in the breeze. Mysterious stirrings were felt in the earth.

Birds appeared and flew into the topmost branches of the trees. Then insects came and butterflies fluttered among the flowers. Then it was the turn of the animals who ran and jumped and crawled in the grass. The earth glowed with colour and the air was filled with music. And into this beautiful world, man himself was born.

As time passed, the serpent god's wounds healed and he grew a new skin the colours of the flowers and birds and plants. It was red and orange, yellow and green, blue and indigo and violet.

One day he looked up at the sky, to his real home beyond the wild roaring river. 'I have made a good and beautiful world,' he said to himself. 'It is time for me to leave it to grow and flourish in its own way.'

So the serpent god coiled his body one last time and sprang like a boomerang across the mountains, through the clouds, up to the sun, over the wild roaring river and down, down to the spirit world on the other side. He sloughed off his rainbow-skin and left it hanging in the sky above the earth. And that, they say, is how rainbows were born.

Chinimin was waiting. Now he was proud of his father who had filled the barren earth with colour. 'I will tell my sons and daughters,' he said. 'And they will pass it on, so that everyone who comes after me will know the story of my father, the Rainbow Serpent, who created the world.'

SPEAKING AND LISTENING

Listening

- Listen to the story of 'The Rainbow Serpent' read aloud. It is a long-ago story in which the Australian Aborigines tried to come to terms with the mysteries of creation. Few of these creation myths were written down, but were passed from one generation to another by word of mouth. At the end of 'The Rainbow Serpent', Chinimin says, *'I will tell the story to my sons and daughters and they will pass it on.'*

- The Aborigines believed in endless Dreamtime where man dreamed fantastic dreams of men and animals as interchangeable beings, for example, the spirit god becoming a serpent. They thought that a 'oneness' existed between men, animals and their environment and that all living creatures were linked in a spiritual relationship. (See *Language activities*.)

Australia

- Find Australia on a world map or the globe. It is the smallest continent in the world. Collect brochures from travel agencies and make up a class resource book about Australia with maps, photographs, places of interest, etc.

Creation stories

- Read the creation story in the Bible, (Genesis, Chapter 1). One version says, *'On the third day God created the dry land which he called the earth and water which he called the sea, and very quickly there were plants and grass and trees with lovely fruits.'* Discuss the similarities and differences between this story and the Aboriginal one. Can you find any more creation stories?

Water

- Many parts of Australia experience prolonged periods of drought. 'The Rainbow Serpent' reminds us of the importance of water in a land where water is a scarce resource. Think of what happens when there is a water shortage: no garden sprinklers, no car washing, no hoses allowed. Sometimes people have to queue to get water in pans and buckets. Talk about the things that you would ban in a water shortage (baths? showers?) and the times when a certain amount of water is essential. (See *Language activities*.)

- Find and read poems about water ('This morning my dad shouted' and 'What is water?' by John Foster, 'Water's for...' by Judith Nicholls). (See *Language activities*.)

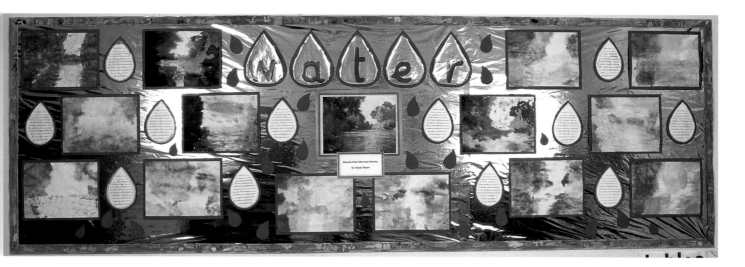

Reptiles

- What is another name for a serpent? Reptiles were evolved from primitive amphibians: most live on land and breathe with lungs, not gills. Most have a dry waterproof skin with scales. How many different reptiles can you name (lizards and snakes, tortoises and turtles, crocodiles and alligators, etc.)? Don't forget to include some dinosaurs, many of which were reptiles.

- Make a class book about reptiles with notes and illustrations. (See *Art activities*.)

LANGUAGE ACTIVITIES

Mini-story
- Tell the story of 'The Rainbow Serpent' in no more than 100 words. Divide it into four parts and make it into a zigzag book.

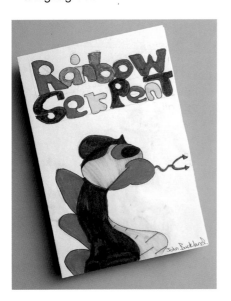

Rainbows
- Write out the seven colours of the rainbow in order. Think of two things that are always red, orange, yellow, etc. The youngest children can make up a rainbow list poem, beginning like this, perhaps:

> *Red is for poppies and blood.*
> *Orange for oranges and juice,*
> *Yellow's for buttercups and dandelions,*
> *Green is for fir trees and grass.........and so on.*

Acrostics
- Another approach is to write an acrostic poem using the initial letters of the word RAINBOW to start each new line of the poem. A very simple poem might look like this:

R ain's
A rch
I s a
N arrow
B ridge
O ver
W ater

Display the poems on a rainbow background using faint lines of coloured pencil.

- Try an acrostic poem about AUSTRALIA.

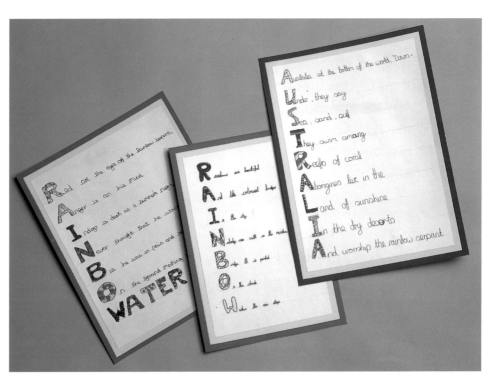

Dreamtime

- When the Aborigines thought about Dreamtime, they dreamed of a mystic relationship between men and animals (see *Speaking and listening*).

- Work on a new Dreamtime story in which someone turns into an animal - and back again. Imagine that you can use magic words, *Abracadabra*, or *Fee, fi, fo, fum!* or a phrase which you have made up, to turn a prince into a frog, a swimmer into a fish, your teacher into a toad, a pirate into a crocodile, and so on. Make your story fantastic and very exciting. Before you start you should try to decide who your story is about (main characters), where it takes place (setting), and what happens (plot). Take time to make these outline notes on scrap paper and use them to help write your final piece.

- Imagine that you can store all the magic elements of Dreamtime, for example, *glistening of the stars, laughing of the waves, music of the mountains,* etc. Put your ideas into a list poem and display it inside a *Dreamtime Box* **(see photograph).**

What is water?

- John Foster's poem of this name begins by thinking of water as a magician. Think of other images to describe water, for example, a bird, a lion, a racehorse, and use these ideas as the basis of a poem of your own.

Each verse should follow a three-line pattern, something like this:

> *Water is a sea-bird*
> *Swooping over cliffs,*
> *Drifting on wings of white spray.*
>
> *Water is a racehorse*
> *Galloping across the sands,*
> *Tossing its mane in the wind.*

The trick of these poems is to fit an appropriate image to the idea of water and to carry it through all three lines. In the first example, we use a set of words, *swooping, drifting, wings,* which connect the bird image to that of the sea **(see photograph).**

Storm clouds

- The serpent god *'sent for the darkest clouds and the strongest winds to create a ferocious storm'*. Make notes on the problems such a storm can bring. Then think through the senses and add more ideas. Use your notes to write a description of the storm for a newspaper or for television. Devise an arresting headline, for example, 'Storm lashes the coast', 'Storm of the century', 'Caravans washed away in storm', etc. Make your descriptive piece very dramatic. Illustrate the newspaper story and make a storyboard for the television version.

If I ruled the world...

- The rainbow serpent was able to build the world to his own design. *'Birds appeared...then insects came...then it was the turn of the animals...'*. Imagine where you would start if you had the same opportunity. Write a story or a report of how you would go about setting up a brand-new world. Where would you start? Is there anything you would leave out? Would things (trees, fruit, rivers, people) look the same or different? If different, in what way? Call the piece, *If I ruled the world,* and set your imagination free!

Shape poems

- Write a short poem about a snake, thinking of colour, movement, shape, and so on. Space the words across the page to make a snake pattern.

> Snake slithers
> across pebbles,
> hides
> in long grass,
> hissing
> with fury,
> forked tongue
> sizzling,
> striped body
> looping
> and coiling
> under the sun.

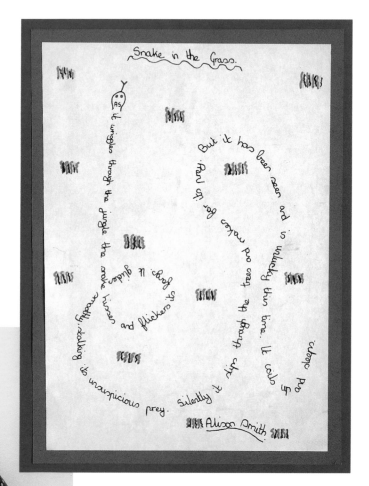

Recipe for Australia

- Think about the things you might associate with Australia: barbecue, surfing, boomerangs, etc. Select words you might find in a cookery book: *mix, whisk, stir,* and so on, to build up a recipe poem, mixing details about Australia with cookbook instructions, as shown.

16

ART ACTIVITIES

Rainbow garden

- *'As water soaked into the earth, plants of every colour appeared like a great patchwork quilt thrown across the land.'* Make a mosaic display panel featuring flowers in a patchwork quilt effect.

- Collect empty seed packets and flower catalogues. Look for illustrated garden articles in magazines and supplements. Cut out lots of individual flowers and leaves, all different sizes and shapes. Put them into sets of colour: red, orange, yellow, green, blue, and so on. Now, on a large backing sheet, block out areas to be filled with one colour. (Be sure to make these large enough to catch the eye.) Then fill each colour panel with cut-out flowers, pasted collage-style, one in yellows, one in reds, and so on. To make an impact, use a variety of shades of each colour. (**See photograph above.**)

Insects and butterflies

- *'Insects came and butterflies fluttered among the flowers.'* Look for butterfly pictures and copy these using felt-tip pens. Work as a group and choose as many different colours and patterns as you can find. Cut the butterflies out. Now make and cut out pictures of wasps, moths, bees and dragonflies. Working in the same way, make flower heads.
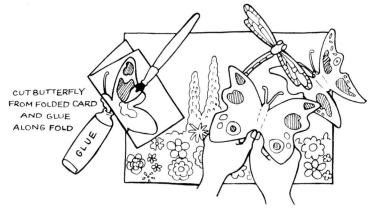
On a blue backing sheet, arrange the row of flower heads along the bottom. Now paste flying insects in profusion across the 'sky'. With the butterflies, moths and dragonflies, glue only the body part, so that the wings appear to fly free of the page.

CUT BUTTERFLY FROM FOLDED CARD AND GLUE ALONG FOLD

GLUE

Hot colours, cold colours

- *'Red flowers sprang from the serpent god's blood, blue from the waters of the river.'* Make patterns or colour wheels using a range of reds (hot colours), and a range of blues (cold colours). Work in two groups. Give one thick ready-mixed red, white and black paint. Give the other group blue, white and black paint. They should also have plenty of clean water, brushes, rags and old saucers or plates.

Demonstrate how to make a tint by putting some red paint on a saucer and adding a little white. Make a shade by mixing a little black paint into the red. Show that the brushes must always be washed and wiped dry before using a new colour. Work in the same way with the blue group. Now make colour wheels or ladders with eight sections and fill in with a range of tints and shades of red/blue. When these groups have finished, let others make patterns, again using only tints and shades of one colour.

Snake patterns

- Look at pictures of snakes/serpents. Look at the patterns on the skin. Using thin card in a dark colour, draw and cut out coiling snakes. Mark out a pattern in stripes or in circles. Now with a variety of pasta, lentils, rice, etc., fill in the patterns on the skin, using a strong PVC paste. Paint a background of pebbles and long grass and paste the decorated snakes in place.

Rainbow serpent

- Design a rainbow serpent using a wax scratch resist technique. Make the snake from overlapping circles. Each circle can be about the size of a saucer. Use thick wax crayon to colour it. Cover with black paint, then scratch off, in a textured line pattern. Paste the circles in place, adding a painted head and fangs. **(See photograph.)**

Lizards, turtles and tortoises

- Use reference books showing pictures of various reptiles. Draw simplified outlines of lizards, turtles and tortoises and fill in these shapes with a variety of collage materials. You might use overlapping shiny green paper for the lizard, string or wool stuck down in circles for the surface of the tortoise shell, pasta or beans to make the turtle shell. Experiment with different colours and textures until you arrive at something interesting and unusual.

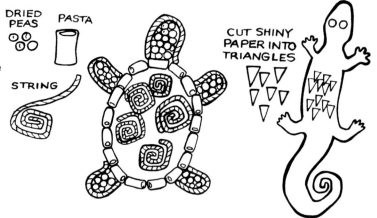

Make a wall of painted stones, a pond and long grass as a background. Cut out the finished reptiles and display them, each in their own environment. Complete with a shiny yellow sun beaming down from the sky.

Summer garden

- *'The earth glowed with colour...'* Create a richly coloured garden by filling your paper end-to-end with strokes and dots of colour. Start with a leafy background, using a variety of greens, dark for shadowy places, light for sunny parts. Blend the greens into one another, stroking the paint in different directions until the paper is covered in a pattern of greens. When it is dry, dot bright flowers all over in red and blue, yellow and orange, pink and purple. Make it into an all-over pattern, not necessarily trying to paint realistic flowers.

A STORY FROM CHINA
The Willow Pattern Story

In the days of long ago, when China was still ruled by Emperors, there was a very rich man called T'so Ling. He had a beautiful daughter, Koong-se. She lived with her father in a palace on the banks of a wide blue river. She had everything that money could buy - lovely clothes, lots of food and servants to look after her. She had a magnificent garden to walk in. It was full of flowers - camellias and poppies and blood-red peonies. But Koong-se was lonely and longed to have a friend to talk with and someone to love her.

One day, when she was walking among the weeping willow trees that grew along the banks of the wide blue river, she felt so sad and lonely that she began to cry. Great tears fell from her eyes and splashed on the ground by her feet.

'Are you trying to water the garden for me?' asked a gentle voice. Koong-se looked up and saw a young man leaning on a hoe among the blood-red peonies. 'I'm sorry,' said Koong-se. 'I thought I was alone.'

'There now, don't cry,' the young man said. 'The sun is riding high in the sky and the wide blue river is singing to you.' Koong-se smiled through her tears. 'Who are you?' she asked. The young man was T'so Ling's new gardener, whose name was Chang. Every day after that, he and Koong-se met under the branches of the weeping willow trees by the wide blue river. They became good friends and had no secrets from one another. Koong-se was no longer lonely.

Summer passed, then autumn, then winter. By then Chang and Koong-se had fallen in love. When T'so Ling found out, he was very angry and sent Chang away. 'You must never meet my daughter again!' he raged. The very next day T'so Ling banished Koong-se to live by herself in a little house on the banks of the wide blue river. He had a high wall built around it so that she could not escape. Nor could Chang climb over.

Soon afterwards, T'so Ling told Koong-se that he had arranged for her to marry a rich man like himself, and just as old. Koong-se was so upset that she couldn't stop crying. She longed to see Chang again. 'When is the wedding to be?' Koong-se asked through her tears. 'In the spring,' said her father, and he gave her a casket of rich jewels which the bridegroom had sent as a wedding present. 'I don't want his jewels,' cried Koong-se, and she hid the casket on a high shelf out of sight.

Koong-se shuddered at the thought of marrying a rich old man whom she had never met. Every day, as the days grew warmer, she watched the buds grow fat and full on the almond tree by the wall and wished that spring would never come. Every day her tears fell ever faster and floated like almond blossom on the waters of the wide blue river.

Like everyone else, Chang heard the bells ring out for Koong-se's wedding. 'It's my last chance!' he thought. So, on the night before the wedding, Chang borrowed a boat and sailed up the wide blue river. He moored the boat under a bridge and quietly made his way to Koong-se's house. At the gate, he called her name very softly, like a bird calling in the night. 'Come quickly,' he whispered. Koong-se heard Chang's voice and came running to meet him. Despite her hurry, she remembered to take the casket of rich jewels with her!

Chang took the casket and grabbed Koong-se's hand and together they raced across the bridge towards the waiting boat. But T'so Ling had been watching from the palace window. He picked up his hunting whip and gave chase, but he soon felt out of breath and couldn't catch the young lovers.

Chang and Koong-se sailed all through the night and next day until they came to an island in the middle of the wide blue river. There they moored their boat and lay down to rest beneath some weeping willow trees. Nobody lived on the island. 'This will be a good place to make our home,' Chang said. They were married in a nearby town where nobody knew them and Chang sold Koong-se's rich jewels to buy what they needed. Chang built a little house and made a garden.

Years passed and they had many sons and daughters who were all very happy. They laughed and sang and played in the wide blue river. But one dark day when the children had gone swimming, Koong-se's father discovered where she and Chang were living. He sent his soldiers to kill them.

The gods knew how much love there had been between Chang and Koong-se, so they turned their spirits into two beautiful doves. To this day, it is said, they still soar and swoop above the branches of the weeping willow trees which grow along the banks of the wild blue river.

SPEAKING AND LISTENING

Listening

- Listen to the story of 'The Willow Pattern' read aloud. If possible, look at a willow-patterned plate and identify the people and places in the story: T'so Ling's house, the river, high wall, the bridge, the island, doves, and so on.

- Divide the children into groups. Invite each to tell part of the story, pointing out the pictures on the plate, as it is passed from one group to another. (See *Language activities.*)

China

- Find China (The People's Republic of China) on a globe or world map. It is an immense area in central and eastern Asia. Can you find and note down the countries which border China?
  Civilisation in China is believed to date from the Xia dynasty (2200-1700 BC), that is, about 2000 years before Jesus was born, so the legend of the Willow Pattern story may be very ancient indeed.

Willow pattern plates

- The distinctive Chinese scene was first brought to Europe and used by the artist Thomas Minton round about 1780. At that time there was a fashion for Chinese art and design. The willow pattern was so admired that it was copied on cups, saucers and plates by many other ceramic factories and was commonly seen on tables throughout the U.K. Can you borrow painted plates or vases with a different pattern and invent a story from the pictures?

The Chinese weeping willow

- Look at books which help to identify common trees. Find pictures of the weeping willow. Why do you think the tree is so named? Trees are said to be 'weeping' if their branches droop and almost touch the ground. (See *Language* and *Art activities.*)

- Make a scrap book of trees which you can identify. Draw the tree in summer and winter. Some trees (deciduous) lose their leaves in winter. Others (evergreen), have needles which keep them looking green all year round. Which kind of tree is the weeping willow?

- You might want to gather fallen leaves and seeds. Fix these on to adhesive tape and stick in position beside the appropriate pictures. Can you find and draw leaves from the weeping willow? Describe the difference in shape between willow leaves and, for example, those of the horse chestnut. Focus this discussion on clear descriptions of the shape, colour and texture of different leaves.

LANGUAGE ACTIVITIES

Blue and white

- Imagine a day when everything you see around you appears to be in blue and white, like the willow pattern plates. You can have a blue and white day in winter, in spring or in summer. Read the poems below and try to decide where the poet was when she wrote them. Think, too, about the time of year.

> *First blue day of the year*
> *grape hyacinths splashed*
> *across grey gardens, high sweet*
> *birds, sky trying on springtime*
> *silks, wind-flowers scattered*
> *like shadows in corners.*

> *Blue and white day,*
> *boats at anchor in the estuary,*
> *   sky marled with cloud.*
> *Willow-pattern plates*
> *on display in the windows*
> *   of antique shops.*

(Two part-poems by Moira Andrew)

- Write a short descriptive poem (6-10 lines, no longer) beginning with the words *Blue and white day...*
  Think about the place and time of year before you start to describe the scene: for example, a snow-covered garden on a sunny winter's day, or a summer sea scene with seagulls and yachts with white sails.

- Try a similar poem beginning *Green and yellow day...* a field of buttercups in June? Or *Grey and silver day...* a misty autumn day, perhaps?

The willow pattern story

- Write a mini-story of Koong-se, Chang and T'so Ling in 100 words. When you are happy with your rough copy, divide it into four parts.

  Cut white drawing-quality paper or thin card into a circle by drawing round a tea-plate. Mark it out into quarters and, using blue ink, write your story, one part to each segment, leaving the outer edge free. You will need to turn the paper round as you write the story.

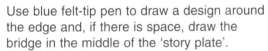

Use blue felt-tip pen to draw a design around the edge and, if there is space, draw the bridge in the middle of the 'story plate'.

Weeping willow

- Look in your tree book or, even better, look outside, for a weeping willow tree. Note the shape, the way the branches droop almost to the ground as though the tree itself was crying with sadness. (See *Speaking and listening*.)

- Think of other images for the willow branches, for example, like a fountain, like the spray from a garden sprinkler, like coiling snakes, like ropes on a jetty, like falling tears, and so on. Once you have collected a number of images, lightly draw a weeping willow tree. Write out one image on each drooping branch, so that you create a shape poem. Finish off the picture-poem in coloured pencil or felt-tip pen.

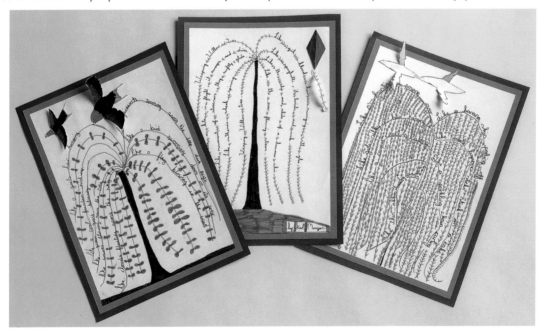

Sad and lonely

- Koong-se felt so sad and lonely that she began to cry. Quietly think about a time when you may have felt upset - after your best friend went away, on the death of a pet, going to a new school where you know no-one, and so on.

- Write down a 'shopping list' of feelings words: sad, upset, scared, lonely, frightened, apprehensive. From these, build up a word-picture which would let the reader into your life, sharing your thoughts and feelings about your sad time. Don't read the piece aloud if you don't want to, but perhaps let the teacher or a best friend read it silently.

Changing places

- Change places with the characters in the story and write Koong-se's story, writing from her point of view. Building on your own experiences of sadness or loneliness, think about how she would feel to be shut up in a small house all alone with the threat of marriage to a man she had never met. Or take Chang's part and write about his feelings when T'so Ling sent him away, with the words, *'You must never meet my daughter again!'*

The escape

- The willow pattern legend tells us that T'so Ling sent his soldiers to kill Koong-se and Chang. Make up a new ending, one in which the family escapes. How? Where did they go? What happened next? Write a happy ending to the story.

What if...

- The gods were sorry for Koong-se and Chang *'so they turned their spirits into two beautiful doves.'* What if you were turned into something different? Imagine what animal or bird you would choose if you could be something else for just one day: a fish, a tiger, an eagle, a lizard? or some other creature?

- Describe a day in your life when, magically, you are transformed into another creature. Imagine what it is like to be able to fly, to swim among the coral reefs, to sit in the sun all day, to climb to the top of the highest tree, and so on. Describe what you do as an animal that you can't do in real life, how it feels to look out from an animal's eyes, how you feel about hunting for food, etc. Finish off by telling about the magic moment when you are back to being your plain ordinary self!

Two beautiful doves

- The story says that two beautiful doves *'still soar and swoop above the branches of the weeping willow trees.'* Write a haiku (in three lines with 5-7-5 syllables in each line), to describe the doves' everlasting flight.

Weeping willow trees
sway over wide blue waters,
where lovers fly free.

Two silky white doves
soar and fly into the air
wings beating in tune.

- Present your haiku as a flap book. Fold art paper or sugar paper into a double zig-zag and write the haiku inside opening flaps. Draw appropriate pictures on the flaps, using felt-tip pens.

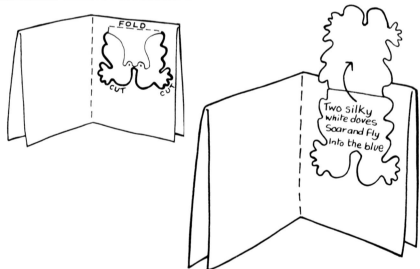

ART ACTIVITIES

Display

- Create a blue and white display using willow pattern plates, blue flowers in a blue vase, blue and white drapes, books, pictures, and so on. Add the blue and white poems to the display panel (see page 20).

T'so Ling's palace

- Look for pictures of Chinese pagodas. These are multi-storeyed towers, each with a roof of glazed tiles. Draw a tall tower and make a window in each storey. Paint the pagoda in a range of blues, from pale (with lots of white paint added) through to quite a dark colour. Cut out an 'opening' window at each level and paste one of the main characters behind it, so that they appear to be looking out.

Painted plates

- Using a tea-plate, cut out a circle on white art paper or thin card. In groups, decide which part of "The Willow Tree Story" you want to paint, so that the story will be complete when all the 'plates' are on show. Use blue, white and black paint to make a range of tints and shades. (Add white to make a tint, a touch of black to make a shade.) Paint your chosen part of the story, all in blue, then make a border pattern round the edge. Arrange a set of 'plates' on the wall to tell the Willow Pattern story in sequence.

  With the youngest children, a quick and easy way of producing these wall pictures is to use paper picnic plates - not quite as satisfying as the 'home-produced' ones, but reasonably effective.

Secret pictures

- Use a white wax crayon or a white candle on white paper to draw scenes from "The Willow Pattern Story". You won't be able to see what you have drawn! Then wash all over the paper with thin blue paint and the wax picture will show up.

Willow tree walk

- Paint, or make a collage of, a tall willow tree to display in the corner of the classroom. Hang your willow images from each branch, like leaves. Add books, plants and pictures to finish off your display **(see photograph)**.

Stencilled Chinese landscape

- Draw and cut out images from "The Willow Pattern Story" on old newspapers or sugar paper. Include the palace, bridge, willow trees, boat, the island, the two birds, etc. Lay these out on drawing paper and spray with pale blue poster paint, using a fine plant spray or one bought from an art shop. When the paint is dry, move every cut-out about 2cm to the left, then respray, this time using a deeper shade of blue paint. You will have a shadowy picture in a mixture of blues with some pure white shapes beneath.

- You can experiment with other complementary colours, making a different landscape - perhaps a mountain scene in shades of purple, or a woodland picture in a variety of greens.

Festival of flowers

- The ancient Chinese had a festival for the Goddess of Flowers when it was the custom for children to make paper flowers to wear. You can imagine Koong-se picking flowers from her magnificent garden, *'camellias and poppies and blood-red peonies'*. Using tissue paper, make flower garlands for Koong-se using a range of reds, pinks and purples. Tear or cut petals and glue at the middle to make flowers. Finish with a yellow centre made from adhesive paper.

Stitch several paper flowers on green garden twine to make garlands.

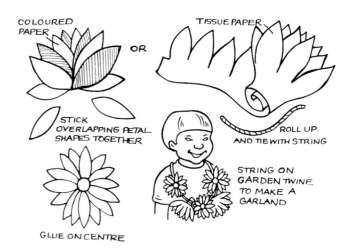

Bird border frieze

- The gods turned Chang and Koong-se into 'two beautiful doves'. Make an unusual and exciting bird frieze by using a chalk and crayon transfer technique to which everyone in the class contributes. **(See display photograph on page 20.)**

First practise by drawing decorative birds, concentrating on line and pattern.

When you are happy with your design, fold a sheet of unlined A4 paper in half. Cover the half-sheet with a thick layer of chalk using several different colours. No white paper should show through. Get rid of the chalk dust, then cover the chalk with two layers of wax crayon, a light-coloured crayon first, followed by a darker one. The wax crayon must cover all traces of the chalk.

Refold the paper, so that the coloured part is covered by the white paper. Pressing down hard, copy your bird design on to the white paper with a pencil. When you have finished, open the fold and your design will appear twice!

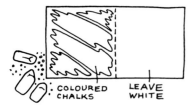

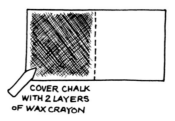

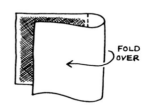

Using the coloured pictures, join them with adhesive tape to make a long continuous border of decorated birds.

A STORY FROM ENGLAND
St George and the Dragon

Once, in days of long ago, when magic still shimmered in the air, dragons were found all over the world. They came in all shapes and sizes. Some little ones lived in the forests and hid beneath stones. Others were as large as steam engines and lived in dark caves in the mountains.

The story goes that there was once a great green dragon with scales of peacock blue and huge blood-red wings. He was one of the fiercest dragons in the world and when he was angry, which was almost all the time, he roared a great roar and breathed a terrible fire. He was always hungry. And, like the true dragon he was, what he liked best of all was a tasty girl-child, a princess for preference.

The dragon lived in a cave on a mountain top near the town of Silne. The townspeople were very afraid of him. They had a meeting to decide how to get rid of him.

When the dragon woke up, he was very hungry indeed, so he roared his great roar and breathed his terrible fire. The townsfolk trembled. 'Let's give the dragon a good meal,' they said to one another. 'Then he might go away and leave us alone!'

So they decided to feed the dragon a fine fat sheep. Two brave young men climbed the mountain, tied the fine fat sheep to a tree and scampered back to the town as fast as their legs would take them. Far from encouraging the dragon to leave, the good meal he had had made him decide to live in the cave on the mountain top for ever and ever. He closed his eyes, wrapped his blood-red wings around him and settled down to sleep.

Next day, the dragon roared his great roar and breathed his terrible fire. Again the townspeople trembled and again they sent two brave young men to the top of the mountain with another fine fat sheep for the dragon's dinner. This went on day after day, until the town ran out of fine fat sheep. 'What will we do now?' the people asked one another.

Then the King had a good idea. 'I know a lot about dragons,' he said. 'They are said to find girl-children very tasty. Perhaps if we feed him a beautiful girl-child, he will go away and leave us in peace!' The townspeople were horrified. 'The dragon won't get my daughter!' they cried. So the King had to think of a fair way of choosing a girl-child for the dragon's next meal. 'I know,' he said. 'We will have a lottery. Every girl in the town will get a ticket. Then we will draw the numbers out of a hat - we'll use my crown, if you like!' So that was decided.

Up in his cave, the dragon was feeling very hungry and getting crosser by the minute. Now his voice was like a thunderstorm, his fire like lightning. 'Where is my dinner?' he roared.

The king organised the lottery as quickly as he could, and when a ticket was pulled from his crown, a beautiful girl-child was torn from her tearful parents and taken up the mountain to be fed to the dragon. He liked the taste very much indeed. 'That was quite delicious,' he said to himself, licking his fiery lips. 'I'm glad I decided to stay.' And so it went on for many months until the town began to run out of girl-children.

One day it was the turn of the princess herself. 'But you can't take my only daughter!' shouted the king. Tears poured down his cheeks and he buried his face in a spotted handkerchief. But the princess said, 'Be brave, father. It's only fair that I should be fed to the dragon too.' So she was led off to the mountain top.

At that very moment, a handsome knight called George rode into town on a milk-white horse. He was hoping to find a fair maiden to ride with him, but saw that there were no girl-children anywhere in town. All the townspeople looked very sad, not a smile amongst them.

George soon found out what had happened, so he galloped up to the mountain top. He found the princess tied to a tree, quite unharmed. The dragon had overslept. George leapt from his milk-white horse and ran to free the princess. At that moment, the dragon awoke. The princess closed her eyes and waited to be eaten up.

But George wasn't afraid. He unsheathed his sword and thrust it at the dragon's peacock-blue throat and the dragon fell down dead. Then he helped the princess on to his horse and they rode back down the mountain to meet the king.

It is said that the townspeople were so delighted with George's brave deed that they did as he said and all became Christians. And George? He was made a saint and, in time, became the patron saint of England.

SPEAKING AND LISTENING

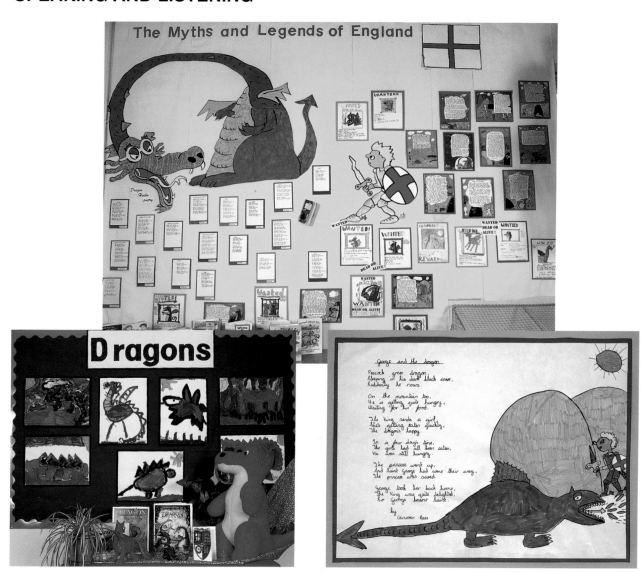

Listening

- Listen to the story of "St George and the Dragon" read aloud. This story is a legend, but George was a real person who lived early in the 4th century. Can you find out more about him?

- St George is the patron saint of England. Can you find the date of St George's day (23rd April)? Do you know, or can you find out about the patron saints of Scotland, Ireland and Wales?

- Talk about the difference between legends and history. Can you think of any other tales which mix truth with fiction? (Think of the stories of King Arthur and the Knights of the Round Table.)

Dragons

- Can you make a picture of the dragon in your head? Can you imagine a small friendly dragon, one who lives in the forest and hides under stones? (See *Language activities.*)

- Look in an illustrated book or draw your own imaginary dragon. Make it as colourful as possible and don't forget to think about his scales and spikes (if he has any!), his tail and wings, and so on. Keep your drawing covered up and don't let anyone see it. Now work with a partner. Stand a hard-backed book between you, so that your partner can't see the dragon picture which you are looking at. Your partner needs a sheet of paper, a pencil and some felt-tip pens or crayons. Then slowly describe your dragon bit by bit. Your partner should try to draw the dragon you have described, just from what you have said. Of course, s/he can ask questions. Then change places. (This task helps children to understand the need for accurate description and helps them to give clear concise instructions.)

- Find poems about dragons and, in a large illustrated floor book, make a dragon anthology for each group. Choose a poem to read aloud to the others, and give reasons for your choice. (See *Dragon Poems*, by John Foster, OUP 1991, and the poem 'A small dragon' by Brian Patten.

LANGUAGE ACTIVITIES

I wish I'd lived in days of old

- Imagine living in days of long ago when, as the story says, *'magic still shimmered in the air and dragons were found all over the world.'* Note down five things that you think you might have enjoyed about those legendary times, and five things you would miss. Put your ideas together to write a short descriptive story or a poem about the days when magic was said to be in the air. (See *Art Activities*.)

- Read Moira Andrew's poem, 'Dragon days', and make up another verse to 'match', that is, using the same first line and making the poem five lines long. You will need to find more words to rhyme with *old*. Try *fold, behold, rolled, sold, mould, scold, twofold, marigold, stronghold...*, and so on.

Dragon days

> I wish I'd lived in days of old
> when dragons were in fashion,
> when knights were brave and bold
> and a puff or two of dragon-fire
> could keep you from the cold.

> I wish I'd lived in days of old
> with magic all the rage,
> with legends still untold,
> when shining swords saved maidens fair
> and streets were paved with gold.

Moira Andrew

- From your list, use the same format to make up a copy-cat poem about the things that you wouldn't like, or things that you would miss if you had lived *in days of old.* For a first line try,
  > I'm glad I live in modern times

You will need to find rhymes for *times*, for example, *rhymes, crimes, pantomimes, daytimes, night-times,* and so on. (You could also use near-rhymes, for example, *shines, pines, mines, lines, underlines,* etc.)

- Write your *days of old* poem behind opening castle doors, and your *modern times* poem on a computer screen.

Dragons

- A small dragon: In the story, it says *"Some little dragons lived in the forests and hid beneath stones."* Imagine a friendly dragon, small enough to hide under stones and fallen leaves in a forest. What colour/size would it be? How would it look? What would it feed on? What would its voice sound like?

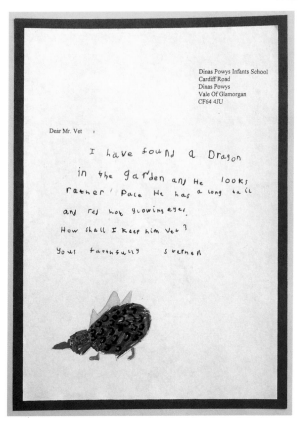

- In Brian Patten's poem, he describes finding a small dragon in the woodshed and trying to find lots of different things that it might like to eat, *"grass, the roots of stars, hazelnuts and dandelion"*, but he can't get it right. Think what might happen if you found a small dragon in a strange place and tried to look after it. Where would it sleep? What would you give it to eat?

- Write a letter to an animal doctor, or a television vet, explaining that you have found a small dragon. You will need to describe it, and ask his advice about looking after it. Set your letter out correctly with your address or the school address at the top.

Here is the news

- Read and think about the St George and the Dragon legend again. Work in two groups, one putting together the story as if you were newspaper reporters, the other a television crew. Give your paper or programme a suitable title, for example, *Silne Times*, or *Tonight's Special Panorama Programme*.

- Think about the people you would want to interview to give your report 'human interest'. Children in other groups can play the parts of characters in the story: various townspeople - the mayor, parents, boys and girls, the King, the princess, George. You, as reporters, should interview them, asking questions about what they saw and heard, how they felt, etc. Make notes.

- Select someone to take the parts of reporter and cameraman, prepared to climb the mountain for a first-hand account of the dragon: description, sounds, how s/he felt on first meeting the dragon face-to-face, 'photographs', etc. (See *Art activities*.)

- Put your completed report into a newspaper format, complete with appropriate headline: DEADLY DRAGON TERRIFIES TOWN, BRAVE KNIGHT RIDES TO RESCUE, or present it as an in-depth investigation, or as a news item.

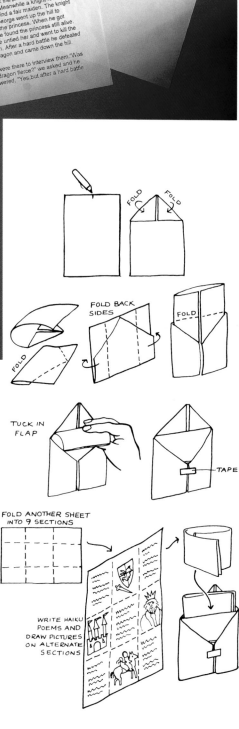

Dragon haiku

- Haiku are very short poems, first imported from Japan. They are written to a very strict pattern, based on syllables. *Cave* has one syllable, *dragon* has two, and *mountain top* has three. Practise first by making syllable groups using your own names, *Jack*, *Saul* and *Kate* are one-syllable names; *Susan*, *Deema* and *Malcolm* two; *Katherine* and *Alison* three. Is there anyone in your group with a four or five syllable name?

A haiku must have seventeen syllables in this order:
> *Peacock green dragon (5)*
> *waits in a dark mountain cave (7)*
> *for a tasty meal. (5)*

Now try making up more haiku to describe the fierce dragon (or a small friendly one), always keeping to the strict syllable pattern. Here are more first lines:

> *See the dragon's fire...*
> *On the mountain top...*
> *Hear the dragon's roar...*

Write the finished haiku on A4 paper, fold it into nine sections **(see photograph above)** and place in an envelope, made origami-style from another A4 sheet. (From an original design by Paul Johnson, in *A Book of One's Own*, Hodder and Stoughton.)

Tell the whole story of St George and the Dragon in a set of haiku as in the photograph. (A set of related haiku is called a *renga*.)

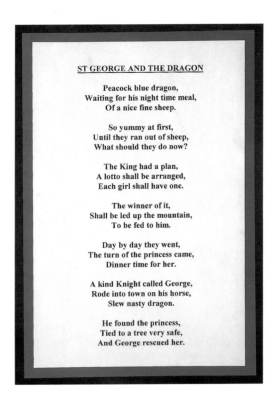

ST GEORGE AND THE DRAGON

Peacock blue dragon,
Waiting for his night time meal,
Of a nice fine sheep.

So yummy at first,
Until they ran out of sheep,
What should they do now?

The King had a plan,
A lotto shall be arranged,
Each girl shall have one.

The winner of it,
Shall be led up the mountain,
To be fed to him.

Day by day they went,
The turn of the princess came,
Dinner time for her.

A kind Knight called George,
Rode into town on his horse,
Slew nasty dragon.

He found the princess,
Tied to a tree very safe,
And George rescued her.

St Henrietta and the unicorn

• Tell a similar story to "St George and the Dragon", but turn all the male characters into women and girls, so that the king becomes the queen, the girl-children become boy-children, and St George becomes a female saint. Make the dragon into a different mythical creature, for example, a unicorn, a phoenix, a griffin or Pegasus, the winged horse.

Change the details as you go along, but base your story on the original tale, so that it follows the correct sequence of events. Write it as a sad story, or a strange one, or make it quite funny.

This new legend can be written out as a wall story, with groups of the youngest children each telling or writing a 'chapter' as the story progresses. Older children can write and illustrate it comic-style, or put it into a self-made concertina book.

The most exciting day of my life!

• Write notes as if you were St George writing in his diary on the most exciting day of his life, the day he rescued the princess from the dragon. Use a simple note form, like this perhaps: *Exciting day. Rode into the town of Silne. Heard about a dragon living on the mountain top. Set out to rescue the King's daughter. Hoped I wouldn't be too late!*

ART ACTIVITIES

Dragon portrait

- Make a large frieze of the dragon, following the colour clues in the story: *a great green dragon with scales of peacock blue and huge blood-red wings.*
  Outline the dragon shape, making it big enough to almost fill a thick card backing sheet.

  Make up some thick 'pudding paint' to the following basic recipe:
  5 cups water
  2 cups plain white flour
  ½ cup sugar
  3 tablespoons salt

  Method: Mix ingredients together in a basin. Pour into a saucepan and cook until thick and bubbling. Cool and store in the fridge. (In covered containers, the mixture will keep for a week or two.) Spoon mixture into small containers and add liquid or powdered poster paint as required, one colour to each container.

  Using the 'pudding paint' mixture, spoon out on to a mixing plate. Use blue and yellow, or a ready-mixed green to make a range of vivid greens. With lolly sticks or thick brushes, fill in the body outline of the dragon with layered strokes of different greens. When it is dry, paint the wings red using the same method.

  Again, leave the painting to dry, then with blue/green/turquoise foil cut into 'leaves', glue on the 'peacock-blue scales', starting from the bottom of the dragon's back and working up. Add red, orange and yellow 'flames' in tissue, crêpe and foil papers.

  You might wish to add a flame-patterned border to finish off the frieze. Books, children's poems and toy or pottery dragons can be arranged below to make an attractive table display. **(See display photograph, page 28.)**

Pennants and shields

- When knights rode into battle, they carried shields with the family coat-of-arms on them. Sometimes they also had pennants or banners with the same design. They were used for recognition, rather in the way football or rugby teams are recognised by the colours and patterns on their shirts.

- Design a pennant or a shield suitable for St George. You might want to think of using the colours (red and white) of the flag of St George. On the other hand, you might go for something flame-coloured with a picture of a milk-white horse painted on it. Copy the outline in the line drawings shown here or have them photocopied and enlarged ready to fill in with your own pattern in felt-tip pens or coloured pencils.

- Try inventing a coat-of-arms for your own family.

- Make very large pennants to hang on a tree in the school playground. (You need to choose a fine day for this, of course!)

I wish I'd lived in days of old

- Ask at home if you may have a photograph of yourself which you are allowed to cut up. Then, working from the poem 'Dragon Days', or your own version of the poem (see *Language activities*), paint or draw an imaginary picture of 'days of old'. You might choose to include pavements paved with gold, knights riding to battle, dragons, castles and princesses. Make it a very busy-looking picture, full of colour.

Make sure that there is room to include yourself in the picture by choosing to take the part of a brave knight, a king, a maiden fair, a wizard or someone else featured in the scene. When your painting is dry, or you have finished using felt-tip pens, carefully cut out the face of the character you have chosen to be. Paste the cut-out photograph of your face looking out into your 'days of old' scene. You might want to spatter the finished picture with gold or silver glitter dabbed in glue to give the picture the finished effect of *'magic still shimmering in the air'*.

A small dragon

- Use clay or salt dough to make a model of a very small dragon, one which *'lives in the forests and hides beneath stones'*. Paint it green or brown, so that it can be camouflaged by the ferns and leaves on the forest floor.

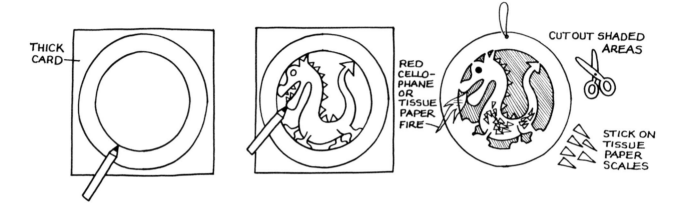

- Using thin card, make a dragon mobile. Use two tea-plates as templates, drawing round the larger one to make the outline, then using the smaller plate for the inner circle. Draw a dragon which touches the inner circle in several places. Under supervision, use a craft knife and a self-sealing board, or sharp-pointed scissors, to cut out the shape. On both sides, decorate the dragon with overlapping paper scales, bright paper 'fire', remembering to give it one large round black eye on each side. Hang from a loop of cotton.

If the class makes several dragon mobiles, each different in colour, size and shape, they can illustrate the opening lines of the story - *'In days of long ago, dragons were found all over the world. They came in all shapes and sizes.'*

All the girl-children in the town

- Make a chain of dancing girls from folded paper. First fold the paper in as many sections as you want figures, then outline very simple shapes, so that hands and skirts touch. Cut out this shape.

Unfold the paper and colour the figures, giving each a different brightly-patterned skirt. You can make the chain more elaborate by gluing on strands of woollen hair and making frilly skirts with either paper doilies or material from the junk box cut out and stuck into place.

Wanted!

- Design a Wanted poster offering a reward for finding (and killing) the dragon. Put his picture in the middle of the poster and make him look very fierce and fiery. Give a full description of what he has done and where he is to be found. The poster should be in bold print, easily read. Don't forget to mention the reward offered. Should it be a bag of gold? Should it be a treasure chest of jewels? Should it be the offer of the princess's hand in marriage? Or what? You must decide.

A STORY FROM GREECE
Flight to the Sun

Icarus and his father, Daedalus, were in trouble - deep trouble. Daedalus had designed a labyrinth for the palace grounds. 'I have made it so complicated that it's impossible for anyone to escape,' he boasted. At first the king was delighted. Then one of his prize prisoners found his way out of the labyrinth and King Minos ordered Daedalus and his son to be thrown into prison.

The king's soldiers bundled Icarus and his father up a winding stone staircase where spiders crawled and rats raced. They pushed their prisoners into a dark cell at the top of the palace tower. Through a narrow window, high in the wall, shone the light of the moon. Icarus shivered. 'We will never escape from here!' he said. 'Perhaps things won't seem so bad in the morning,' said Daedalus. So they ate some bread and lay down together on a thin mattress. Icarus dreamed of home.

Day after day they had only bread to eat and water to drink. Icarus was hungry and bored. The guards didn't talk and his father was too busy planning an escape to say a lot.

So Icarus made friends with some bees who built their hive in a corner of the window. He listened to them buzzing, and watched as they flew back and forth bringing pollen from the flowers. 'I wish we could fly like the bees,' he said.

Icarus made friends with the birds who perched on the window ledge of the cell. He watched them swinging and swooping in the sunshine. 'I wish we could fly like the birds,' he said to Daedalus. 'Then we could escape!'

Daedalus thought about the birds and the bees. 'Icarus, I have a plan', he said. 'First, we must feed the birds every day.' So Icarus collected all the bits of left-over bread and scattered crumbs on the window ledge. More and more birds came. Soon the window ledge was covered in feathers.

'Gather up all the feathers you can find,' Daedalus said. 'Then sort them out, small soft ones here, thick strong ones over there. Then I want you to collect wax from the bees and bring it to me.' Icarus did as he was told, but couldn't think what Daedalus was going to do with the feathers. 'It's not as though we can fly!' he said. 'Be patient,' said Daedalus, so Icarus watched and waited.

Daedalus shaped the birds' feathers into wings. He held them in place with wax from the bees. When the guards came with their food, they hid the wings under the mattress. Every day Daedalus made the wings bigger and more powerful.

One morning, before the guards were awake, Daedalus said to Icarus, 'Come and try your wings.' He tore a strip of cotton from the hem of his robe and tied the smaller wings on Icarus's back. Icarus was very excited. Daedalus tied the other pair of wings to his own back. 'We are nearly ready, said Daedalus. 'But first I want you to listen carefully. Don't fly too near the sea or your wings will get wet, and don't fly too near the sun or the wax will melt.' 'Yes, yes, father,' said Icarus who didn't want to listen to a long lecture. He climbed out on to the window sill. He could feel the warmth of the sun and the cool breeze on his face. 'Hurry, father,' he called. Daedalus struggled to the ledge. 'Follow me,' he said to Icarus. 'Go where I go and do what I do - nothing else! Good luck!'

Daedalus closed his eyes and jumped. He flapped his wings. 'My plan is working!' he thought. He looked round for Icarus, who was swinging and swooping through the air. 'Watch me, father,' he called. 'I can fly like a bird!' He soared up to meet Daedalus.

'Don't show off,' said Daedalus. But Icarus wasn't listening. He flew down to touch the wave tops, flew up again just as he felt the cool spray on his cheeks. 'This is wonderful!' he shouted. Icarus flew on up and up into the air. 'Not too high,' called Daedalus, but his voice was lost in the sound of the sea. 'Come back, Icarus!' he shouted.

Icarus felt the heat of the sun on his face. He felt his cheeks begin to burn. Then his wings touched the sun. Too late, Icarus remembered what his father had said. The wax began to melt. He went into a deep dive to get away from the heat, but his wings fell to bits about him. A few soft feathers drifted past his face. He tried to beat what was left of his wings, but it was no good. Down, down to the ocean he fell, feathers fluttering about him like white rose petals in a summer wind.

Daedalus heard the boy's screams as he fell. 'Icarus,' he called. 'Why didn't you listen?' But there was nothing he could do. In his heart he grieved for his son, but on he flew until he landed safely on the shores of Sicily.

SPEAKING AND LISTENING

Listening

- Listen to the story of Icarus read aloud. Listen to poems about flying, for example, 'Sometimes' by Phil Carradice, and 'Balloon fiesta', by Moira Andrew.

- Look for more Greek stories and legends in the school library. In groups, choose one story to read to the other children in the class. Discuss which story is most interesting and why. Look at the illustrations and talk about the clothes and other details.

All about Greece

- Find out where Greece is on the globe or on a world map. Pinpoint the main towns, rivers and islands.

- Look in the school or class library for interesting facts about Greece. Collect books and holiday brochures. Listen to children who may have been on holiday on the Greek islands. Ask them to tell what the weather/houses/food was like.

Flying high

- Icarus went *'swinging and swooping'* like a bird. Discuss other creatures which can fly: butterflies, dragonflies, ladybirds, moths, and so on. Now search for more unusual flying creatures, perhaps those of pre-history, such as the pterodactyl. Think of creatures in fables: Pegasus, griffins, dragons. Think of seeds that fly: sycamore, dandelions, Old Man's Beard, thistles, etc. (See *Language/Art activities.*)

- Talk about how it must feel to be able to fly, to see the world from a different angle, looking down on rooftops, the tops of trees, clouds, church spires, and so on. (See *Language* and *Art*.)

- Encourage the children to build an oral thesaurus of 'flying' words: *fluttering, swooping, gliding, soaring, spinning, hovering.* (See *Language activities.*)

Sometimes parents know best!

- Discuss how Icarus responded to his father's advice. Why didn't he listen? What was he trying to do? Talk about what can happen when children show off.

- Discuss when it is essential to listen to what adults say and to obey, for example, crossing at a safe place on the road. What other safety messages are important? Gather ideas to make a *Keep safe* poster. (See *Art activities.*)

LANGUAGE ACTIVITIES

Mini-story

- Write a mini-story about Icarus using no more than 100 words. Keeping the sequence of events, divide the story into four sections, for example, Icarus and Daedalus in prison, making wings, learning to fly, going too near the sun.

- Expand each idea into a paragraph of the story - in only 25 words. Make an four-page illustrated zigzag book with the title on the cover.

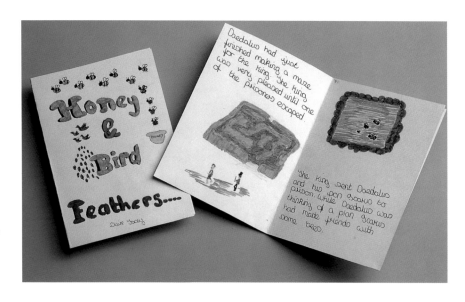

I wish I could fly!

- When Icarus saw the birds and the bees, he said, *'I wish we could fly!'* Imagine what that would be like. Write down the names of all the flying creatures that you can remember. Think about different 'flying words'. (See *Speaking and listening.*) For the youngest children, make simple list poems, based on wishes. In the examples shown here, six-year-olds have been encouraged to explore and exploit a range of language possibilities.

Decorate the border of your poems with flying creatures. Give them a 3D look by pasting down only the body of the insect, with the wings flying free **(see photograph).**

- With older children, suggest that they write about where they would like to fly: *above the trees, over the hills, beyond the river, through the clouds,* and so on. Use these ideas as 'building blocks' for a poem, expanding each into a new verse. Suggest a title, such as *If I had wings.* Make the poem into a layered mobile. **(See photograph.)**

37

The day I got lost

• Have you ever been lost?...in the supermarket, on the beach, in an unfamiliar street, in a theme park, in a maze? Talk about the experiences in your group. Find five words to express how you felt (or might have felt). Try to put the *feeling* words in order, for example, *worried, nervous, frightened, panic-stricken, terrified...*

Think about the people and things you saw about you, the sounds you heard, what went through your head. Write what happened as a page in your diary, for example, *Monday 4th August, in Majorca/Blackpool/Bristol/London.*

Lost in the labyrinth

• Using your own experience of being lost, imagine that you are a prisoner of King Minos, trapped in the labyrinth that Daedalus built. Write a page of the prisoner's diary, expressing his fear, his frustration at coming up against another dead end, another stone wall, another hedge just like the last. Think and write about how he would look up at the sun, at the birds flying free. Think and write about the sounds he might hear.

• Experiment with ways of making the prisoner's diary look ancient - brown ink on torn paper, perhaps - and write a page which might have been smuggled out to a friend on the outside of the maze.

You never listen!

• Daedalus warned Icarus not to go too near the sun, but Icarus didn't listen! Have you ever been told not to do something, gone ahead and got into trouble? Read 'Don't you dare!' and make up your own poem, following a similar pattern.

'Don't you dare!' said Mum
But I did. I dared.
I ate all the plums that
were in the fruit basket.
'I feel sick,' I said.
'Serves you right!' said Mum.
*   'You never listen!'*

'Don't you dare!' said Dad.
But I did. I dared.
I turned on the outside tap
and cold water squirted out.
'I'm wet through,' I said.
'Whose fault is that?' said Dad.
*   'You never listen!'*

Moira Andrew

• You might add a verse for Icarus. *'Don't fly too near the sun!'* said Dad, but Icarus did. He flew too high...and so on.

The sun

- Talk with the children about why Icarus fell out of the sky. Talk about the heat of the sun. Think about what fierce sunshine can do to your skin. Make a collection of 'hot' verbs: *burns, dazzles, scorches,* and so on. Use these to make a list poem about the heat of the sun.

- Write the sun poems into sun-shapes cut from yellow card. Using red and orange tissue paper or felt-tip pens, make rays to back the sun poems.

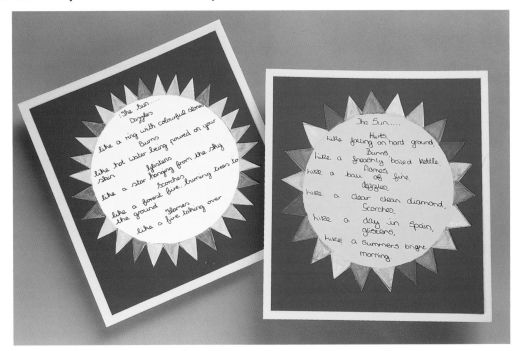

Flying seeds

- Look in the school garden or the park to find seeds that float or fly. Failing this, copy flying seed illustrations from tree and wildflower books. (See *Speaking and listening*.) Make a reference book for your seeds (about A5 is a suitable size). Press your seeds under heavy books. When they are dried, use adhesive-backed clearfilm to display them in the book. Name each seed and draw pictures of the tree or flower which will, in time, grow from the flying seed.

- Make a class set of seed books and invite children from a different class, or parents, to read and learn from them.

- Find out different ways in which the seeds are made to fly. For example, poppy seeds are shaken out from a 'pepperpot' head, sycamore seeds twirl on 'wings', and so on. Using your discoveries, make up a flying seed poem. It might begin like this:

> *Poppy seeds are shaken*
> *like pepper from a pot.*
> *Sycamores float like*
> *dragonflies on the wind.*

Decorate the finished poem with a frame of flying seeds.

Magic carpet

- Discuss the idea of a magic carpet. Ask children to describe where they would wish to ride if tickets on a magic carpet were free. Imagine flying near the moon, among the creatures of the night. Suggest that they think about the feel of the wind in their hair, how the world would look from the air.

- Using some of these ideas, write a magic carpet story, each group perhaps taking a new chapter. Make it into a long wall story.

ART ACTIVITIES

Magic carpet

- Make a long frieze with cut-out silhouettes of rooftops, treetops, mountain tops, church spires, etc., in shades of grey, with a few black shapes to give definition.

Ask children to paint owls, bats, flying leaves and a bright white moon. (If you imagine flying across far-off countries you might include the tops of minarets, palm trees, pyramids, etc.)

- Paint or use felt-tip pens to make an elaborately-decorated magic carpet. Cut out and add child figures to ride on it. Glue one or more magic carpets to the night sky of the silhouette frieze. (See *Language activities*.)

Flight to the Sun

- On a pale blue background, make a sea and sunshine frieze to complement the night frieze above. Use cut paper shapes for the waves, layering greens on blues and silver. Make a huge round sun, using vivid yellow paint. Surround it with rays using reds, oranges and different yellows in crêpe paper or tissue paper, again using a layering technique.

GLUE FEATHERS ON FROM EDGE OF WING AND WORK BACKWARDS

- Paint large figures of Icarus and Daedalus in white robes. Give them huge feathered wings using overlapping white tissue paper or crêpe paper (see cover) leaf shapes, starting from the bottom and working up.

Glue the cut-out figures in the sky with Icarus almost touching the sun. This frieze can be used as a background to an 'All about Greece' display, where books, maps and Greek holiday brochures, etc., are available. (See *Language activities*.)

Beehive mobile

- Cut brown card into overlapping strips as shown and make them into the shape of a hive. Use felt-tip pens to draw any number of brightly-striped bees. Cut out. Use 20-30cm of fine wire, and tape to the backs of the bees. Fix the other end behind the hive so that it looks as if the bees are flying back and forth *'bringing pollen from the flowers'*. Hang the mobile from beams or from the ceiling. (Should there be a problem with the school alarm system, glue corks to the back of the hive and display against a blue background, so that the 'bees' fly free.)

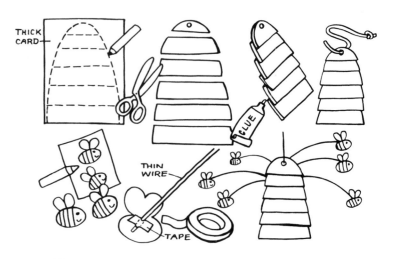

THICK CARD

THIN WIRE

TAPE

Wax resist

- Daedalus used wax to hold the wing feathers in place. Talk about how wax is used, for example, to preserve cheese, to make polish, to make candles, and so on.

- Make decorated wax resist sea patterns to cover books telling the story of Icarus. On white paper, use a white candle or wax crayon to make a very thick wavy pattern. Brush over with thin paint in bright blues or greens and the white waves will show up. When the sea pattern is dry, stick a round yellow or golden sun-shape in place.

Secret letters

- Red wax was once used to seal secret or important letters. Why do you think this was? What do we use now? Have you ever seen documents sealed in red wax?

- Many people had a special seal designed for their use alone. It often showed a family crest or the initials of the sender. Design your own 'seal' using Plasticine and you can send a secret letter.

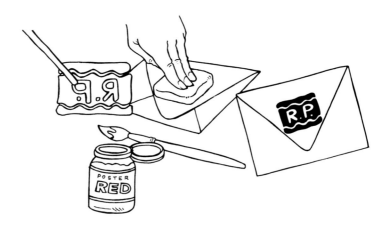

- Using white paper, make an envelope, and glue the tabs into place at the back. Cut paper to fit and write a secret letter to slip inside.

- Shape some Plasticine into a square block and make a pattern (or press out your initials) by pressing a stick into the Plasticine. Put some red poster paint or ink on a plate and press the Plasticine block, pattern side down, on to it. Use the Plasticine block to print your personal 'seal' on the back of the envelope.

Keep safe

- Paint posters to reinforce the times when it is essential to do what parents and other adults tell you. (See *Speaking and listening.*) List some of the very important things that they say, for example, *Don't play with fire! Cross the road at a safe place! Don't talk to strangers! Swim where it is safe!*

- Make a poster for each idea using only the minimum number of words to get your message across. It can look very effective if you edge the posters with an appropriate pattern, for example, flames for the fire message, sparks for *Don't play with fireworks!*, waves for a safe swimming poster.

Flying high

- Look in reference books for pictures of flying dinosaurs or for mythical beasts with wings. (See *Speaking and listening.*) In a group, paint and cut out fairly large pictures of some of these creatures. In addition, you may like to invent new winged beasts of your own. When the pictures are dry, cut out and glue, collage-style, on a background of sky, clouds and sun, or of night, moon and stars, to make an exciting *Flying high* frieze.

A STORY FROM INDIA
The Great Storm

Manu lived by himself in a hut by the river. Sometimes he felt lonely with nobody to talk to all day. 'I wish I had a friend,' he sighed. But there was no answer, just the silence of the blue hills and the chuckling of the river.

Around his hut, Manu had a beautiful garden, full of flowers and trees. But it was so hot under the yellow eye of the sun that Manu had to go down to the river every day for water to keep his garden green and beautiful.

One day, as he knelt by the river to fill a jar with water, Manu saw a tiny golden fish. On its head, it had a slender spike. Manu had never seen a fish like it. To his surprise, the fish said, 'Manu, you look lonely. Would you be willing to look after me and be my friend?'

'What a good idea!' said Manu, and he scooped up the tiny fish and carried him home in the jar. As Manu was getting ready for bed that night, he heard the fish say, 'You have saved my life, Manu! I will never forget your kindness.'

When Manu woke next morning, he could hardly believe his eyes. The tiny golden fish had grown to the size of a skate. His body filled the jar and his head was pushed right out into the air. He gasped for breath. 'Save me, Manu,' he called.

Quickly Manu filled a tin bath with water from the river and slipped the fish into it. The fish swam around, his golden spike gleaming in the sunshine. 'You have saved my life again, Manu!' he said.

But by the following morning, the fish had grown to the size of a whale. Water slopped over the sides of the tin bath. Again the fish was gasping for breath, so Manu ran with him as fast as he could to the village pond. 'Thank you, Manu. You have saved my life again,' said the fish. 'Please come and see me every day.'
So every day, Manu went to the village pond to talk to his friend.

And every day the fish grew bigger. Soon he would be too big for the pond. 'Will you take me to the sea, Manu?' he asked. By now the fish was too heavy to carry and much too big to fit on his wheelbarrow, so Manu made a plan.

He dug and dug all through the night. By morning he was exhausted, but he had dug a channel deep enough for the huge golden fish to swim in. 'Come on, my friend. Swim to the sea. The ocean is big and deep and wide. There will be enough room there, no matter how big you grow!' Manu was sad to see his friend swim away. The hut seemed lonelier than ever and even the beautiful garden didn't make him feel very happy.

Some time later, crowds of excited villagers ran past his hut. 'We are going down to the sea,' they said. They told Manu that a huge golden fish had been sighted swimming near the shore. It was so enormous that everyone wanted to see it with their own eyes.

Manu wondered if it could be his long-lost friend, so he hurried down to the shore. Sure enough, Manu saw that the enormous golden fish had a spike on its head. He found a boat and rowed out across the green waves to meet him.

Bobbing behind his friend, Manu saw a magnificent sailing ship with red sails flapping in the wind. 'Manu, my friend,' called the fish. 'Four times you saved my life. Now it is my turn to look after you. Soon a great storm will flood the land. Nothing will be left alive! So, gather two of every bird and creature and find as many different plants as you can and bring them to the ship. But hurry!'

So Manu collected plants from his garden and asked two of every kind of animal and bird to come with him. Soon they were all aboard the ship. Manu told the villagers what the fish had said. 'Get down to your boats,' he told them. 'Soon a great storm will destroy the land!' But the villagers just laughed. 'Poor Manu,' they said. 'He's been on his own too long.'

Just one beautiful young girl listened. 'May I come with you, Manu?' she asked. 'Yes,' said Manu and they climbed aboard the ship as the first drops of rain started to fall.

Soon the wind blew cold and strong. The waves grew deep and dark and the ship was tossed up in the air and down again. Then the golden fish appeared. 'Don't be afraid, Manu,' he called above the noise of the storm. 'Throw the mooring rope over my spike and I will tow you to safety.' And he did.

Manu and the beautiful young girl made a new life together after the storm. They planted a new garden where animals grazed and birds nested in the trees. And Manu was never lonely again.

SPEAKING AND LISTENING

The Great Storm. On a
background of wavy stripes,
paste a cut-out ship and
golden fish, collage-style

Listening
- Listen to the story of 'The
Great Storm' read aloud.
Does it remind you of other
similar stories?

- Find, read and talk about
poems which describe a
fierce storm, for example,
'Giants upstairs' by Stanley
Cook, 'Predator' by Moira
Andrew, 'Thunder and
lightning' by James Kirkup.
Look at the way the poems
are written, and the words
and images which the poets
have chosen. Make a class
anthology of storm poems,
copied in best writing or
word-processed and
illustrated. (See *Language
activities.*)

Noah's ark
- Find and read about Noah and the flood in the Bible (Genesis, Chapters 7 and 8). Talk about similarities
and differences between the stories of Noah and Manu.

- Find books about Noah's Ark and look at how different storytellers approach the same tale. Read a version
of the story of Noah's Ark aloud to your group. In groups, pool your ideas and try to decide which version
you think is most interesting, and why.

- Talk about different ways in which authors write about the same subject. Look, for example, at the story of
Noah written with very young children in mind. How does it differ from a story intended for older children: in
the language used? number of words? illustrations? Discuss what these differences mean for children's
writers. (See *Language activities.*)

India
- Find where the Republic of India is on a world map or on a globe. It is a huge country, over a million
square miles, divided into thirty-one states and territories. There are more than 300 million people living
there, so growing enough food is difficult. Most of the land has to be farmed. Grain, rice, tea and spices
are the main crops. Manu's garden would be very important to him, especially if he grew vegetables as
well as flowers. Try to find out what kinds of vegetables would grow in an Indian garden. (Some are the
same as ours: cabbage, green beans, beetroot, cauliflower, etc. Others are more exotic: aubergine, okra,
etc.)

- Look for recipe books about Indian cooking. Cooking styles vary from one region to another and many Indians are vegetarians. What people can eat sometimes depends on their religion, but most of the recipes use spices and chillies. Have you ever eaten out in an Indian restaurant? Which Indian dish do you like best? Make a bar chart showing which Indian foods members of the class like best.

Spices

- Make a collection of Indian spices, naming them and saying what special taste each has. (Some spices are very hot, so just take the tiniest speck on your fingertip to taste!) The spices in glass jars can look very pretty. Make an Indian foods display with recipe books and spices. Arrange them on a colourful Indian sari. You might be able to ask a teacher or parent to help with making a special Indian meal.

LANGUAGE ACTIVITIES

Noah's ark

- Gather together a number of early reading books. Look at the ways the stories are written, number of pages used, type size, number of words on a page, the illustrations, etc. Write the story of Noah's ark in a style suitable for children who are just learning to read (no more than eight pages, including a title page). Try to write your story in approximately 150 words, with up to 20 words per page.

- Make your story into an illustrated book, leaving lots of room for the artwork. (You might use a computer or word-processor for this.) When your book is completed, read your story aloud to a group of infant children. (See *Art activities*.)

My imaginary friend

- In 'The Great Storm' it says, *'Sometimes Manu felt lonely with nobody to talk to all day.'* Imagine that you are all alone, no brothers, no sisters, no friends. Think about how you would feel. Invent an ideal friend and write about him, her, or even it.

- Take time to think about a really interesting friend. It might be someone who is very like you, almost a twin, or someone who is always getting into trouble, but gets off because s/he is invisible; or, you might like to have a creature from another world as a friend. Make notes about your friend's looks, size, shape, age perhaps. Note what s/he would like to eat, to talk about, to do in and out of school.

- From your notes, write a 'portrait' in words of your imaginary friend. Using faint pencil crayon, draw and colour a picture beneath the writing. Frame the finished piece as though it is a painting, and display a gallery of class portraits. **(See photograph.)**

A fishy tale
- Fishermen are often accused of exaggerating the size of their catch. Write 'a fishy tale', one which is so outrageous that no reader will believe it! You could tell of a fisherman catching a fish the size of a whale in a stream at the bottom of the garden; the Man in the Moon fishing for stars and catching a doorknob; a fishing boat's crew finding a talking fish with a spike on its head among their cod and halibut and hake...or any 'fishy' story of your own choosing. Try to make it unreal, magical or simply funny.

Manu's ship
- With the youngest children, make a zigzag book telling the story of Manu gathering together two of each kind of animal and bird.

> *Manu led birds and animals to the ship,*
> *two grey elephants lumbering*
> *two bright parrots flying*
> *two stripey snakes slithering...*

and so on, keeping to the pattern shown above. Take a page to every new pair of creatures, and illustrate. On the last page, they reach the safety of the ship. *'The wind blew. The rain came, but Manu and the animals sailed away'*. Show the ship and the golden fish in a stormy sea.

The Great Storm
- Gather a set of images to describe the wind, thinking of how the wind sounds and moves as a storm is brewing. Think first of animal images: a bear, a lion, an eagle, a wolf. You might move on to think of the wind as a ghost or an evil spirit because of its invisibility, leaving only destruction in its wake. Choose the most effective image and work on it, putting together matching sounds and movements, for example:

> *The wind is an evil spirit*
> *haunting field and forest,*
> *petrifying with its cold breath*
> *every last living creature.*

Or try,
> *The wind is a grizzly bear*
> *growling a deadly warning,*
> *as it lumbers through forests*
> *leaving destruction in its tracks.*

• Use image to write about a storm at sea where, for example, grey waves ripple like giant reptiles, a storm whips the waves into a demon dance. You can continue with such images or work on different ideas of your own.

Wind poems

• The youngest children can also use image to write about the wind, for example:

*The wind is like a horse
galloping across the sky.
It is like a fierce lion
growling in the night.*

Follow this simple pattern to produce four-line poems which can be displayed on banners looped across a picture of whipped-up waves in blues, greens and silver, or on the sails of a windmill. **(See photograph on the right.)**

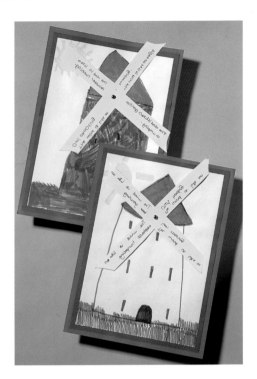

Watch Manu's fish grow

• Write a diary of a fish/bird/animal/child growing from something smaller than your thumbnail into a giant. Imagine the difficulties of being very small indeed (likely to get lost in a pocket or down a drain). Imagine the fun of being able to hide easily (under a teacup, or in your school lunchbox).

• Contrast this with growing to giant proportions, again thinking of the difficulties (getting clothes to fit, always having to bend to get through a door - or, like the fish in the story, finding a pond large enough to swim in). Imagine good things about being a giant (seeing over the crowd at a football match, being able to walk a mile in a minute - or, like the fish, being able to tow a ship out to sea).

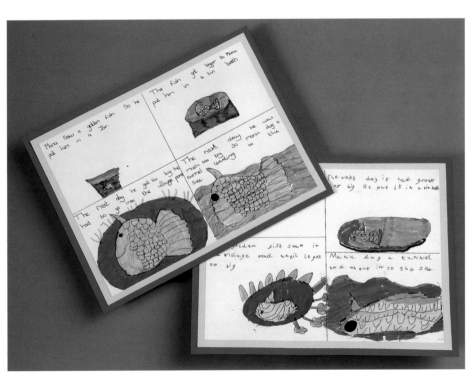

• Using felt-tip pen, show the growth of the fish in four stages: in the jar, bath, pond, ocean. For the youngest children, use a comic-strip technique. For older ones, hang 'the growing fish' pictures on a ribbon. **(See photographs at left and top left.)**

ART ACTIVITIES

Noah's Ark
- Using thin card doubled, draw and cut out an ark shape. On the top sheet, make opening windows or portholes. Then glue the two sheets around the edge. Open the windows and draw pairs of creatures inside each space. Mr and Mrs Noah can be seen inside the opening wheelhouse. Colour the top sheet brown with nail holes to look as though the ark is made of wood. Make each an individual presentation with the cut-out ark sailing into a fierce storm at sea, with great dark waves and lots of rain lashing down.

Manu's sailing ship
- This can be assembled in a similar way, adding bright red sails to the ship. Mount on a stormy background with the golden fish towing the ship out to sea. **(See photograph on page 43.)**

- To extend this idea, make it into a story book, telling the story of either 'Noah's ark' or 'Manu's ship'. (See *Language activities*.) Older children can write for their younger colleagues, making an 'opening book' in the outline shape of ark or ship.

Manu's magic garden
- Design a magical garden for Manu and his beautiful bride. Look for pictures, paintings and photographs of trees and flowers painted in the Indian style. You will see how often the trees and flowers are patterned, looking fantastic and magical, not realistic. **(See illustration on page 4.)**

- To make a magical garden, cut out tree shapes in silver or gold paper. Make leaves and fruit look like jewels, using scraps of shiny wrapping paper, perhaps adding sequins and beads. Fill the foreground of your picture with flower shapes, again using foil papers, sticking them, collage-style, one on top of another so that no backing paper shows through **(see photograph above).**

Down to the sea

- On a roll of lining paper or frieze paper, paint or draw a background for the 'The Great Storm' story. Use all the clues given in the story, for example, *'blue hills and a chuckling river'*. Imagine that you are standing on top of a blue hill and that you can see views all around.

- You will need to show Manu's hut and garden, the river, the pond and the sea. Draw and cut out the sailing ship and the enormous golden fish. These should be pasted on the waves.

- Now make a collection of stand-up animals in pairs: elephants, crocodiles, giraffes, bears, and so on. Each group can decide to work on different animals. To make each animal, fold in half a piece of stiff paper or thin card. Draw the animal so that part of its body is along the fold. Cut round the animal shape, except where it touches the fold. Using felt-tip pens, give the animals stripes, spots or zigzags and mark in eyes, teeth, and so on.

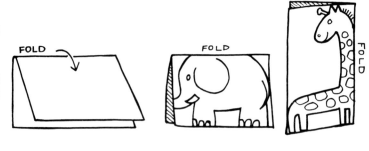

- Now stand the completed animals in front of the story background, as though they were marching down to the sea. Add stand-up figures of Manu and the beautiful girl. This makes an interesting class display, especially for the youngest children.

In the river

- Use a paper batik technique to make an effective display of Manu's *'chuckling river'* alive with fish. Each child should draw a fish in thick wax crayon, almost filling an A4 sheet of cartridge paper. No paper should show through the design. Make all the fish different and quite individual in colour and design.

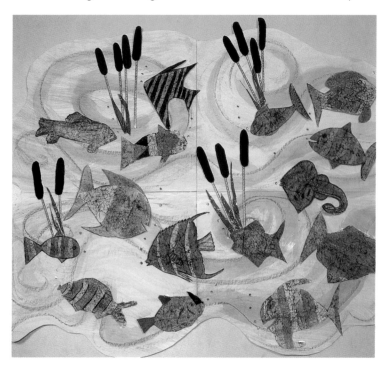

When each picture is finished, screw it up into a ball (as though you were going to throw it away!) and the thick wax will crack. Now smooth out the paper, taking care to blow away any bits of crayon dust. Add a layer of ink or water-based dye in a dark colour, brushing over to make sure that the cracks in the wax are filled with ink. Blot surplus ink with a paper towel.

When the pictures are dry, finish off by pressing with a warm iron between two clean sheets of paper on a wad of old newspapers. This technique gives the fish pictures an interesting texture, rather like scales.

Cut out the fish shapes and glue, collage-style, on a winding blue river. Add some dark rocks and green banks, and weeds or bulrushes.

A STORY FROM NORTH AMERICA
The Night Moon-Woman was Angry

One cold dark night, when clouds drifted across the sky like ships on a stormy sea, Moon-Woman looked down to the dark mountain far below.

On the mountain top, she saw two brothers with bows and arrows. They were called Great Bear and Little Bear. She heard one boast, 'We are the best shooters in the tribe! We can shoot a feather from a sleeping bird, or a cone from the top of the tallest pine tree!' 'And we can hunt on the darkest night!' said his brother.

'Look at the spots on the face of the moon!' said Great Bear. 'Have you ever seen anything so ugly?' 'No, never,' said Little Bear. 'Let's use the ugly old thing for target practice.' With that, he fitted an arrow to his bow and, like a gust of wind, it shot into the night sky and straight to the face of the moon. At that very moment, the stars went out and the moon herself disappeared behind the clouds.

Now it was really dark, dark as the inside of the deepest cave. 'The dark doesn't frighten me,' said Great Bear. 'How about you, Little Bear?' But Little Bear didn't answer. There was nothing but the black silence of a frosty night on the top of the tall dark mountain. Great Bear was all alone. 'Hey, Little Bear, where have you gone?' Great Bear shouted into the black silence. Then the stars lit up again and the moon sailed into view and, from far away, he heard the sound of Little Bear calling.

'Moon-Woman is angry. She has stolen me away. Help! Help!' 'Don't worry, Little Bear,' shouted his brother. 'I'll find a way to rescue you.' So he made a plan. He took careful aim and shot an arrow into the sky. This time the arrow did not touch the moon. It did not touch the stars, but it did wound the darkness, piercing the cold night sky. And there it stayed.

Great Bear took another arrow and another and another, until his quiver was quite empty. Each arrow pierced the one before until they made a long ladder, reaching from the cold night sky right down to the top of the tall dark mountain.

Great Bear put a rope round his waist. Then he picked lots of ripe red berries, as many as he could cram into his pockets. By this time, dawn was breaking. Great Bear went to the bottom of the arrow ladder. He looked up to the sun-streaked sky. Then he began to climb. He climbed for two days and two nights. When he got hungry, he ate some ripe red berries. When he got tired, he tied himself to the arrow ladder with the rope and was rocked to sleep by the wind. When he reached the top he heard a girl's voice. 'Hurry, Great Bear,' she said. 'Moon-Woman is being very cruel to your brother.'

The girl showed Great Bear the path to Moon-Woman's house. She gave him four magic gifts: a pine-cone, a tree-root, a rose and a jagged stone. 'You must find out how to use the magic gifts for yourself,' she said. 'Then come back and I'll show you the way home.'

Soon he saw the round silver moon glimmering and glittering. He heard Moon-Woman shouting and Little Bear crying. Great Bear knocked on the door of the moon. Then he jumped on to the roof. When Moon-Woman opened the door she saw no-one. 'I know you're there!' she called. 'Wait till I get hold of you!'

Great Bear leaned down the chimney and pulled his brother up on to the silver roof. Then they ran across the sky with the speed of the wind. But Moon-Woman ran after them. So Great Bear threw down the magic pine cone and it began to cry with Little Bear's voice.

'Don't play tricks on me', shouted Moon-Woman as she almost caught up with them. Great Bear and Little Bear ran on. They threw down the magic tree-root and it grew into a tree, but Moon-Woman jumped right over it. They threw down the magic rose and at once it grew into a prickly hedge, but Moon-Woman struggled through it. The brothers could hear her close behind them. So Great Bear threw down the magic stone. It grew and grew until it became a mountain, all covered in snow and ice. This was too much for Moon-Woman, who slipped and slithered all the way back to her silver house.

Then the girl appeared on the path. 'Follow me,' she said. 'I'll take you back to the arrow-ladder.' And she did. The brothers thanked her and slid all the way down to the top of the mountain. When they got back to the village, the people of the tribe were so pleased to see them that they held a great feast in their honour.

49

SPEAKING AND LISTENING

Listening

- Listen to 'The Night Moon-Woman was Angry' read aloud. Think about the part of the world in which the brothers Great Bear and Little Bear lived. The original inhabitants of the United States of America and of Canada were Native Americans.

- Find and listen to poems about the moon and poems of the night read aloud. Decide which poems you like best, thinking of, for example, description, feelings, magic, and so on. Copy out and illustrate some of the poems in a large floor book.

Dark places

- In the story it says, *'Now it was dark, dark as the inside of the deepest cave.'* Think of the darkest place you know, for example, under the stairs, your bedroom in the middle of the night, lost in a deep forest, and so on. Talk about how you feel in a dark place - frightened, excited, lonely. (See *Language activities*.)

Stargazers

- Look for books on astronomy in the library. Find out as much as you can about the stars: the names of the constellations and where they are to be found in the night sky.

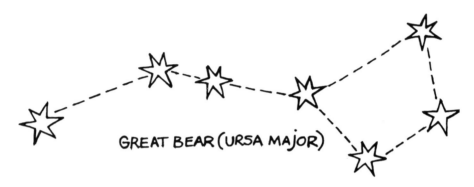

GREAT BEAR (URSA MAJOR)

Talk about the shapes and patterns the constellations make, and invent new names to fit each star-pattern. Look, for example, at the shape of 'the Plough' or 'Great Bear'. Do you think it looks like either? In your groups, try to find more appropriate descriptions.

The first moon landing

- Find out about the first moon landing (Apollo, 20th July, 1969). Discuss how the crew, Neil Armstrong and Edwin (Buzz) Aldrin, must have felt to be the very first people to step on the surface of the moon. Neil Armstrong said, 'One short step for man, one giant leap for mankind.' How would *you* have felt? What message would you have sent to the waiting world? In black pen on white strips of paper, write out your short messages of triumph (no more than 10 words) and paste them criss-cross against a black background.

Native Americans

- There were many different Native American tribes, each with its own cultures, traditions and language. The story of Moon-Woman comes from the Tlingit tribe who lived on the northwest coast of Canada. Every tribe had its own religion, but all shared a belief that everything in the natural world had its own spirit: sun and moon; mountains, rocks and rivers; plants and animals. Above all, the Native American tribes worshipped Mother Earth as the source of everything that was good and beautiful.

- Discuss how you imagine the spirits of sun, moon or stars might look. What kind of voice might they have? What colours would they wear? (See *Language activities*.)

Magic gifts

- The girl in the sky gave Great Bear four magic gifts for luck, *'a pine-cone, a tree-root, a rose and a jagged stone.'* Can you think of other things that are supposed to bring good luck? Think back to the story and retell it with four different magic gifts, for example, *a black cat, a horse-shoe, a four-leafed clover, a falling star* - or any other ideas of your own.

- The magic rose grew into a prickly hedge, the magic tree-root grew into a tall tree, etc. Each magic gift turned into a trap for the Moon-Woman, so imagine how your new good luck gifts would make life difficult for her.

LANGUAGE ACTIVITIES

What is night?

- The story says that the night was *'dark, dark as the deepest cave.'* Note down other images for night, for example: space, a box, a forest, a castle, the cupboard under the stairs, and so on. To make your image into a poem, find an adjective to go with your idea, thinking of colour, feelings, sounds, etc. If night is like space it might be like *outer* space, *swirling* space, *shadowy* space. Try to extend the original image using related words and ideas, always remembering that you are describing night.

- Using different images for night, write mini-poems of three lines each, following the pattern suggested below.

Night is like outer space,
where stars wheel and spin
along pot-holed paths.

Night is like a haunted castle
where ghost-shadows dance
in empty halls.

- Find similar images for the moon. Is the moon like a pearl? a white rose? a silver boat? a grumpy face? Use the same three-line format to make up more mini-poems of the night. Display the poems on a night-time frieze of silhouetted mountains and pine trees against a huge white or silver moon.

Prayer to the moon

- The Native Americans believed that everything in the natural world had its own spirit. (See *Speaking and listening*.) Sometimes they prayed for rain or for sunshine to help make their crops grow. An ancient prayer to the sun begins like this:

  Give me my blue sky for ever,
  ancient man with the lit face.

        (from a translation by Roger Garfitt)

  You might continue this prayer, every second line beginning with the words, *'Give me...'*

- Now make up a new prayer to the moon, again in two-line stanzas. The Native Americans have named the sun *'ancient man with the lit face'*. Think about how they might have described the moon, for example, *'old woman with the silver smile'*, or *'ancient lady with the angry face'*. Now think about what they would want the moon to bring to their world. As before, begin every second line with the words 'Give me...' or 'Give us...' Like this, perhaps **(see following page):**

51

Prayer to the moon

*Give us tides in the sea for ever
old woman with the silver smile.
Give us light in our darkness
old woman with the flickering lamp.*

See text on previous page

- Write your moon prayers in silver pen on circles of black card, and hang on different lengths of cotton across the assembly hall to make a prayer mobile.

Star shapes

- The youngest children can make up simple star poems, again using image. First encourage them to 'trade ideas' orally, perhaps collecting their images on the board. Is a star like a jewel? a snowflake? a teardrop? a daisy petal?

Star shapes

A star is like a snowflake
    drifting in the sky.
It is like a teardrop
    falling down night's face.

Put some of the children's images together, using the above simple pattern. For maximum effect, encourage the children to match the movement word, *drifting, falling, gliding,* to the image they have chosen. (See also *Art activities.*)

Little Bear's story

- For the youngest children, make a zigzag book, four pages long. Encourage their participation in preparing a storyboard from Little Bear's point of view. Arrange the story in four sections.

- Use a combination of words and pin-men characters for the storyboard. This technique helps young children to sequence events as they occur in the story and enables them to visualise the ending.

- When the children come to write their version of the story, encourage them to work from the storyboard, so that each part of the narrative is written on a separate page with appropriate illustrations.

Through Moon-Woman's window

- In the story it says only that Moon-Woman *'.....looked down to the dark mountain far below.'* There is no other description of the land where Great Bear and Little Bear learned to hunt. Imagine for yourself what the land might have looked like and what else Moon-Woman might have seen from her home in the sky. Did she see deep dark rivers, dense pine forests, snowcapped mountains? Did she see animals fleeing from the hunters? the village in which the brothers lived?

- Write as if you were Moon-Woman looking down from your silver window on the land far below. Describe what you can see, the sounds you can hear on the wind, the movements of the animals, birds and people. (See *Art activities.*)

The darkest night

- List all the words you can find for black (you might like to use a thesaurus for this): *sable, ebony, inky, jet,* and so on.

- Read 'Night' by Moira Andrew (see page 2), and look carefully at the penultimate verse:

> *I tell beads of blackness;*
> *sloe, raven, jet, ebony.*
> *Bat-dark depths entice me.*

This part of the poem simply lists some words for darkness. Use your own list to make up similar verses to describe the darkest night, or the moon and stars.

Begin your poem like this:
'Now the night is really dark,
.....'
and put into three-line verses
(see photograph).

Ladders

- Great Bear made a magic ladder leading to the night sky. Make a list of people who use ladders in their jobs: firefighters, steeplejacks, chimneysweeps, crane drivers, etc.

- Describe an apprentice's first day climbing to the top of a factory chimney/the roof of a burning building/to the cab of a crane, etc. Think of the excitement, the fear, trying not to look down, how you (as the new recruit) feel at finally reaching the top, seeing the familiar world below from a new perspective.

- You might also write about Great Bear's ladder adventure, using similar ideas about height, fear, excitement, and so on. Describe looking down on forests and mountain tops, trees looking like green feathers perhaps, rivers like silver threads, etc.

Recipe for magic

- Make a collection of beach pebbles or stones. Imagine that each stone has magic powers. (What would those be? What would you like to happen by magic?) Write out instructions using a recipe format. Ideas should be as exciting and zany as you can make them!

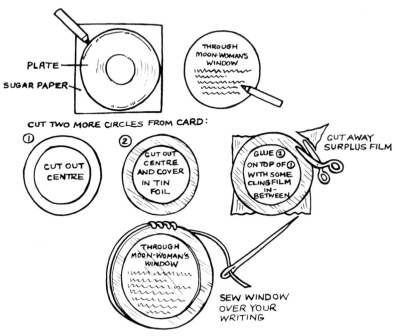

ART ACTIVITIES

Through Moon-Woman's window

(See *Language activities*)

- On white art or sugar paper, draw round a plate, large enough to take your poem or story, and cut it out. Copy your writing out in best on the round shape. In card, cut out two matching circles. Now cut out the centre of each so that you have a 'porthole' effect.

  Cover the second circle with foil, and glue clearfilm between the two, trimming off any surplus film. Now staple or sew the 'window' over your writing, so that it can be read. This makes an unusual round one-poem book, *Through Moon-woman's window*. **(See photographs on facing page.)**

Dark as the darkest night

• Make a 'wash-off' night-time sky background for displaying poems about moon, stars or darkness. To do this, draw a very faint pattern of moon and stars, planets and comets, on a sheet of thick white paper, cut to size. Paint over the moon/star patterns in white poster paint. Using a sponge, try dabbing white poster paint at random to make the Milky Way. Then leave the poster paint to dry out completely.

• Now cover everything - the paper and the white poster paint - with black waterproof ink. Leave to dry. When the ink is dry, hold the paper under a running tap and gently rub it with your hand. The poster paint will wash away, leaving the rest of the picture black, *'dark as the darkest night'*. Lay it flat to dry out, finishing off under some heavy books.

Display the night-time poems on the star-patterned background.

Magic stones

- Design and paint your own version of a 'magic' stone. You need to use a smooth flat stone. Wash the stone and leave it to dry. Draw out a rough idea of your picture or pattern on paper before you begin. Using thick poster paint, paint a base colour all over the stone (purple or a star pattern for a night scene, blue for a mountain picture or forest pattern, green for a North American Indian feather pattern, etc.). With your rough to help you, draw the details of your pattern or picture in pencil. Then paint, using one colour at a time and leaving to dry before you use another. When the picture is finished, it can be coated with clear varnish.

Put your painted stones on display with the other 'magic gifts': the rose, the root and the pine-cone.

Spirits of Mother Earth

- Many of the Native Americans believed that everything in the natural world had its own spirit. (See *Speaking and listening.*) Imagine what the spirit of an eagle, a flower, a deer, etc., might look like. What about spirits for rain or snow, thunder or sunshine? Think about colour and shape. Rough out some ideas on paper, trying to capture the essence of the creature or weather.

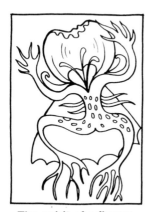  

| The spirit of a flower | The spirit of an eagle | The spirit of lightning |

- Design a wall of 'spirits' by using a wax resist technique. From your rough, draw a variety of spirit pictures in thick bright wax crayon on good paper. For the best results, keep to bold shapes. Using thick dark-coloured paint, go over the wax design. It will resist the paint and leave vivid pictures. Cut these out, leaving a border of dark paint, and display them, glued collage-style, on a backing sheet. Hang the prayer mobiles above the spirit collage.

Star shapes

(See *Language activities*)

- An excellent way of showing the youngest children's star shape poems to advantage is to make them into simple one-poem books. Using white blotting paper or other absorbent paper, cut double circles, large enough to take the poem.

To decorate the cover, use a water-based black felt-tip pen to draw a star shape. Now drip water on the star and, as the water spreads, it will make the black ink split into rainbow colours. Write the poem on a circle, smaller than the blotting paper, and glue to the inside 'page'. Staple the cover and the poem, so that you open the book to read the poem.

Once, when the world was young, the King and Queen of the Sea lived in a deep dark kingdom beneath the waves. They had many beautiful children, all with deep dark eyes and long brown hair. The sea-children were very happy. They sang and made music and the deep dark waves echoed to their songs.

Then one sad day the Sea-Queen died. The sea-children stopped singing and the deep dark waves went quiet. Then the Sea-King found a new wife who promised to look after the sea-children as if they were her own. But in no time at all, she broke her promise. She made a magic potion and gave it to the sea-children to drink. Slowly, they turned into slender seals with brown silken coats and deep dark eyes.

The Sea-King watched with tears in his eyes as the seals who used to be his sea-children swam away to cold grey waters where he could not follow. Yet the magic was not perfect. For just one day in the year, the sea-children could shed their seal-skins and be themselves again.

One day when it was time to go back to being themselves, the sea-children seals swam ashore to a lonely Scottish island. They slipped off their silken skins and played by the water's edge.

Roderick was a fisherman who lived in a cottage by the shore. As he trudged back from a night's fishing, he found a pile of silken seal-skins. He took one home and hid it on a high shelf above the cottage door.

That night, as he mended his nets by the fire, Roderick heard the sound of a sad sweet song like a sea-bird trapped in a net. He went outside and saw a beautiful young woman standing there. 'Please help me,' she said. 'I am a lost sea-child and nowhere can I find my silken seal-skin. I can't go back to the cold grey waters without it.' And she shivered in the cool night air.

Roderick gave her his tartan plaid and sat her by the dying fire. He said nothing about the silken seal-skin which he had hidden above the cottage door. The young woman was so beautiful that he fell in love with her and asked her to marry him.

Roderick and his beautiful seal-wife had many beautiful children who all had sleek brown hair and deep dark eyes like their mother. And for all those years, Roderick kept the secret of the seal-skin hidden above the door. But the Sea-King's daughter was never truly happy. Sometimes, when her husband was out fishing, she wandered along the shore, listening to the music of the waves. Sometimes she caught sight of the slender silken bodies of her brothers and sisters. 'Come back, sea-sister, come back,' they called. And, with all her heart, she wished that she could join them.

One evening there was a great storm, but Roderick had to go fishing in the cold grey waters. In the cottage on the shore, his family slept peacefully - all except the youngest and most beautiful child who crept out into the raging night. As the cottage door banged behind him, the dusty seal-skin fell from its hiding place, so he put it over his shoulders. 'This old blanket will keep me warm in the winter wind,' he said to himself.

The boy's mother woke. When she found that her youngest and most beautiful child had gone, she ran outside, calling his name. She found him standing by the water's edge, watching some sleek brown seals swimming close to the shore. 'Come and join us,' they called. 'Come and be a sea-child as your mother once was.'

At that moment his mother ran up and folded him close in her arms. 'Don't go,' she said. 'You belong in the mortal world. It is I who should go - if only I could find what I lost so long ago.' The youngest and most beautiful child gave the seal-skin to his mother who took him by the hand and led him home. Then she kissed her sleeping children and stepped back out into the raging night. She felt as though her heart was being torn in two, but the call of the sea was strong. She took off her mortal clothes and left them on the shore. Then she pulled on the silken seal-skin and swam off to join her brothers and sisters in the cold grey waters.

When Roderick returned home next morning, he felt very sad to find his beautiful wife gone. He wished with all his heart that he had turned back when the storm broke. He told his children the secret of the long-lost seal-skin and promised to love and care for them all of his days.

Once a year, until the youngest and most beautiful child grew up, the seal-mother slipped off her seal-skin and returned to the cottage by the shore. And in the evening, as the sun slipped down the sky, she kissed her husband and children goodbye and swam off into the cold grey waters, singing in her high sweet voice as she went.

SPEAKING AND LISTENING

Listening

- Listen to the story of 'The Seal-Wife' read aloud. How does it make you feel? If you were to draw pictures of this story, what colours do you think you would use most? Why? Are they *feeling* colours, *weather* colours, *sea* colours? Or some of each? (See *Art activities.*)

- Ask one group to retell the story to the others. At a given signal (the teacher or a member of another group should hold up a STOP! sign), the storyteller must stop and pass on the narrative to the person sitting next to them. Encourage the children to retell the story in their own words, keeping to the correct sequence. It is an effective way of helping children to interact with an audience.

- Look in the school or class library for poems about the sea, about seals, about Scotland or Scottish islands. Read the poems aloud in your groups and talk about why you have chosen them. You might make a class anthology of poems to go with the story of 'The Seal-Wife'.

Islands

- *'The sea-children seals swam ashore to a lonely Scottish island.'* Talk about living on an island. What sights and sounds and inconveniences would make it special? Talk about how you would get to school. Talk about how you would feel to be surrounded by the sea.

- Find out if anyone has visited a Scottish island on holiday. Ask them to tell how they got there (boat, car, plane), what there was to do, what the island looked like. For example, some Scottish islands are almost treeless. Collect holiday brochures and photographs.

- Find Scotland on a road map. Make a list of the names of Scottish islands (see *Language activities*). Make up a rhythmic rap, using some of the island names, for example:
    Mull, Coll, Tiree, Eigg,   Rum, Colonsay, Scalpay, Skye.

- Working in groups, turn the rap into a round, each group starting one after the other, but keeping the rhythm going. You might like to set the island round to music.

Seals

- Find out all you can about seals, where they live, what they like to eat, how they move. They look so graceful in water, so clumsy on land. Why do you think this is? Make drawings, find facts and photographs about seals to make a class book. Some children may have visited the Seal Sanctuary in Cornwall, where injured seals are cared for.

Fishing

- *'Roderick was a fisherman...'* Discuss the hardships and dangers of such a way of life. Listen to children who can tell about visits to a fishing harbour or a lifeboat station. Can you find stories about fishermen?

- Find and read poems about fishing, for example, 'Fishing' by Dave Calder, 'At peace', by Felix Redmill.

Roderick went to sea

- Think about the names of different kinds of fish which we can eat - by looking up a resource book on fish, or by reading from a recipe book. Following the pattern of the old party game, each child in the group takes a turn. This game helps to build children's listening skills. The first child says, *'Roderick went to sea and he caught a sole.'* 'The next says, *'Roderick went to sea and he caught a sole and a haddock.'* Then *'....he caught a sole and a haddock and an eel.'* *'....a sole, a haddock, an eel and an old boot.'* ...and so on.

- Using a reference book on fish, follow up by making a fish frieze with mini-poems. (See *Language* and *Art activities.*)

LANGUAGE ACTIVITIES

Underwater fun and games

- The sea-children were excellent swimmers. Imagine that you can swim and play underwater. Imagine riding on the back of a seahorse, somersaulting in and out of a coral reef, playing hide-and-seek in underwater caves. Using some of these ideas and some of your own, write a story or a poem about the games a sea-child might play.

- The youngest children can set an underwater games poem to the pattern and tune of 'Here we go round the Mulberry Bush' **(as shown in the photograph)**.

Magic potions

- In some versions of 'The Seal-Wife', the Sea-King's new wife was said to be a Sea-witch. Perhaps that is why she was able to make a magic potion to give to the sea-children. Talk about how you could make up such a magic drink (if you were a sea-witch!) using, for example, sea-berries, sea slugs, oysters and so on. Try writing out instructions for a magic potion using a recipe format.

To do this, look up some recipes for making summer drinks. Following the headings, for example, *take, mix, blend,* etc., make up a recipe for the Sea-witch's magic potion, using 'ingredients' from the sea and shore. Make it as horrible/exciting/magical as you can!

The day that changed my life

- Go over 'The Seal-Wife' story in your head. Make notes on what it tells you about Roderick's way of life; what his job was, where he lived, and so on. Use your imagination to fill in more details. What did he look like? How did he feel? What could he see/hear on the wild island shore?

- Write a page of Roderick's autobiography: that is, as if you were Roderick himself. Describe the day that changed his life. Remember to include what he saw and heard, and how he felt. It might begin like this: *I was feeling very tired. I had been fishing all night long. In my basket I had five fresh fish for supper and I was feeling hungry. I'm always on the look-out for useful things washed up on the shore. Imagine my surprise when I found a silken seal-skin. But that wasn't all...*

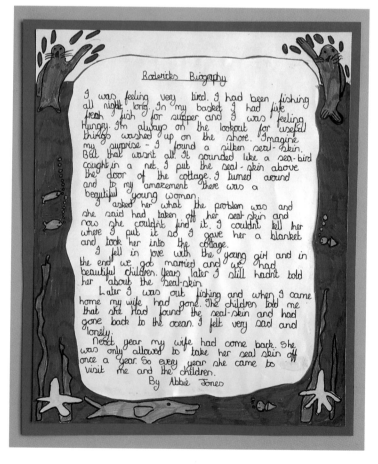

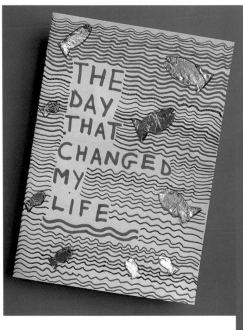

- Or, write your autobiographical story inside an illustrated simple-fold book. Give your book an appropriate title. Frame the cover with a wave pattern and cut-out foil fish.

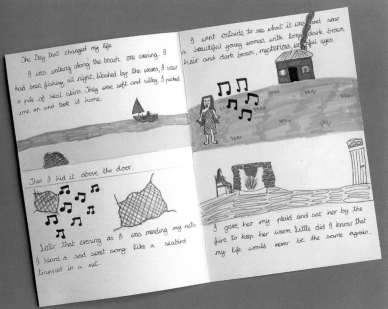

- Think of a special day when your own life was changed in some way, for example, the day your baby brother or sister was born, the day you went to a new school or moved house, or the day you ended up in hospital. Think of how you felt, the things you saw and heard around you.

- Use your first sentence to get your reader right into the story. You might begin with: *It began as just an ordinary day, but....., or: As soon as I woke I knew that this was no ordinary day, or: Nothing had changed. The wardrobe and the window were still in the same place, but the sounds were wrong somehow. I wondered what had happened.* Make this story part of your autobiography.

Roderick went to sea

- Follow up the memory game by looking at the shapes and colours of different kinds of fish. Write mini-poems (no more than five lines) describing each fish. Every child in the group can write one mini-poem.

> *A silver mackerel*
> *glinting*
> *like an underwater dragonfly*
> *stares*
> *from its moon-round eye.*

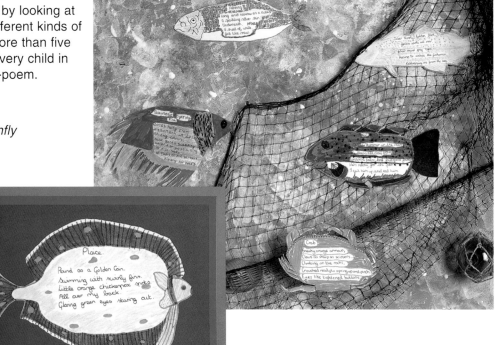

Write out the poem on a fish shape, cut out and glue in place on a piece of netting.

Letters home

- The seal-wife had once been a sea-child, daughter to the Sea-King himself. Perhaps she would write letters home to tell her father what her new life was like. How would she describe the cottage in which she now lived? What would she say about Roderick? She would want to tell her father all about their *'many beautiful children'* (the Sea-King's grandchildren!), what they looked like, what they liked to do, how they behaved, and so on. You might like to think up names for the children.

  Using some of these ideas, write the seal-wife's letter home. Set it out as a real letter, like the one in the photograph.

- Your letters might be very different, but it is important to think yourselves 'into the seal-wife's skin', how she feels, what she sees and hears around her. You might want to write a letter to the old Sea-King from Roderick, saying how happy he is with his beautiful wife and children; or later, how much he misses his seal-wife.

Beachcomber

- A beachcomber looks for 'treasure' washed up on the shore. Think about things you may have found on the beach: shells, driftwood, empty bottles, an old boot, and so on.

  It is important not to pick up anything that looks dangerous, but sometimes people find interesting bits and pieces that they can use for picture-making or sculpture, or to build a fire.

Think of the bits of debris which Roderick might have found on the shore in one week. Write a list poem about how he might have used them.

*On Monday, I found
a dozen shells,
made of them a necklace
for my pretty wife.*

*On Tuesday I found
knotted driftwood,
made it into a rocking horse
for my youngest son.*

> ...and so on.

Treasure island

- The island where the seal-wife landed was surrounded by *'cold grey waters'*. Imagine landing on a different island set in sparkling blue seas. Instead of rocks and a stone-covered shore there might be golden sands, blazing sunshine, palm trees. Imagine being shipwrecked on a tropical island, looking for food and shelter - perhaps finding treasure! In your groups, talk about an island adventure and write a story or a poem.

- You may want to write and illustrate a book of your own, but you could decide to make it a group effort, with one person starting the adventure off, then others working on succeeding chapters.

Island poems

- Using a road atlas, make a list of Scottish islands with unusual names. (See *Speaking and Listening*.) Use the names as the basis for fun poems which rely on alliteration, for example:

> *Amorous ants amble round Arran.*
> *Ridiculous red rhinos romp across Rhum.*
> *Terrible ten-toed toads tramp over Tiree.*
> *Shadowy sharks shiver in Shetland seas.*
>
> ...and so on.

Even those who don't much enjoy writing like tackling these verses! Display on an outline map of Scotland with four or five lines glued into position on the appropriate islands.

ART ACTIVITIES

Treasure islands

- Draw a picture map of your treasure island, marking all its special features. (See *Language Activities*.) Show where wrecks lie beneath the waves. Name the caves, mountains, beaches, rivers, etc. You might indicate where pirates have landed, where treasure might be hidden, etc.

Add a poem to the island picture to give it an extra dimension **(see photograph)**.

Seal-children at play

- Discuss the idea that 'The Seal-Wife' story might make you feel sad. What colours might express this mood? What colours are best to suggest the sea? (See *Speaking and Listening*.)

- Let the children experiment with colour-mixing, using watercolour paints. Encourage them to mix a range of blues, purples, greens and greys. Make wave-shaped patterns using a range of cold colours, five shades of blue or five shades of green.

Using some of these cold sad sea colours, make a 'crystal colour' seascape as a background to a seal-wife display. To do this, take a large sheet of good quality white paper. 'Paint' it with clear water. While it is still wet, use thick brushes to paint fairly large areas of blue, purple and green. Let the colours spread and blend into one another. Work as quickly as you can to cover the paper with pools of sea colours.

Then take a piece of plastic bubble wrap (about twice as big as the background paper), and crumple it. Lay it over the wet painting, pressing it down gently. Leave it to dry overnight. When you remove the plastic next day, you will find an interesting texture in frosted 'crystal colour'. Add cut-out seals, collage-style, swimming and somersaulting through the waves.

- Experiment with coloured inks and bubble wrap or printing with dried seaweed. This makes an unusual book cover, or wrapping paper - especially suitable for a present from the seaside. Pin the seascape behind a seal-wife table display. Use driftwood, shells and stones, books by Scottish poets and writers, postcards and photographs, perhaps adding a tartan scarf and a bunch of dried heather.

The Sea-King's palace
- Imagine how splendid the Sea-King's underwater palace would be - made from shells or coral or coloured stones, perhaps.

Try making a picture of the palace using only dots. Firstly lightly sketch in the outline with chalk (remember to give it ramparts and turrets). Then go over the outline with a cotton bud dipped in paint, using a new bud for each new colour. Fill in the shapes with more dots, until it looks almost solid, but gives the impression of a palace built with hundreds of shells or stones.

When it is dry, add drifting seaweed, using the same technique. Then, again using only cotton buds and dots, draw and paint lots of brightly-coloured fish in all shapes and sizes. Cut them out and paste into position floating in and out of the seaweed and over and around the Sea-King's palace.

Once, in days of long ago, a shepherd and his wife lived in a stone cottage high in the mountains of Wales. They had no children, but they had a flock of black-faced sheep that skipped across the hillsides like mountain goats. Morgan the shepherd, and his wife Bethan, were very happy with their black-faced sheep and their stone cottage, and wanted for nothing.

Morgan was devoted to his sheep and went out in all weathers to make sure they came to no harm. Bethan looked after their newborn lambs, rocking the poorly ones and singing to them as if they were her own babies.

In the long evenings Bethan played her harp and sang in her soft sweet voice. She and Morgan laughed a lot together, especially when he tried to sing, because he had the voice of a raven and not one note of music could he coax from his thick deep throat.

Sometimes when Bethan sang and played, Morgan wished he could join in. Although he tended the sheep with big gentle hands, Morgan's fingers were as thick as sausages and not one note of music could he coax from the fine high harp-strings. Sometimes his neighbour Evan Jones, the tenor, laughed at him. 'Not one note of music has that Morgan Preece in his whole body!'

One night, when Bethan had gone to sing with the chapel choir and Morgan was alone by the cottage fire, there was a knock on the door. 'Who can this be?' he said to himself. 'No travellers ever pass this way, high on the Welsh mountains.' When Morgan opened the door he saw three wizened little men, in green coats, standing outside. 'Good evening,' they said. 'We have come a long way and we are hungry and tired. Could you spare a bite of food and a drop of ale?'

Morgan opened the cottage door wide. 'Come in,' he said. 'My wife baked a cake this very day, so I can offer you bread and cheese and a slice of cake.' He poured mugs of ale and sat the three little men down by the fire. When they had finished their supper, one of the little men said, 'We'd like to thank you, Morgan Preece, so tell me, what does your heart desire?' Morgan said, 'I have just one wish. I wish I could play the harp. My wife Bethan plays like an angel.'

'Say no more,' said the little man and there, in the hearth, stood a shining golden harp. 'Just one thing,' said the little man. 'Never play with spite in your heart!' 'No, never,' promised Morgan, with eyes as wide as windows. But the three wizened little men in their green coats had vanished.

Morgan sat by the dying fire. He ran his thick fingers over the strings and music rippled like mountain waters from the shining golden harp. When Bethan came home he was still playing and she could not believe her ears. Then Bethan began to dance to Morgan's music. She danced in and out of the door, up and down the stairs, round the table and round the chairs. She grew very tired, but she couldn't stop. 'Stop, Morgan! Stop!' she called. 'If you play, then I must dance!' So Morgan put down the shining golden harp and immediately the music stopped. Bethan sank into a chair, quite exhausted.

The people of the valley soon heard about the magic music in the stone cottage on the high mountain. 'Will you play for us, Morgan Preece?' they asked. So Morgan took down the shining golden harp and played until everyone joined in the dance and the air was filled with music. But Morgan always stopped before they got too tired.

One day, when Bethan had gone to chapel, there was a knock on the door. Evan Jones, the tenor, stood in the doorway. He said, 'I know you can't coax one note of music from your throat, let alone from the strings of a harp, so why do you tell people you can play? You are a liar, Morgan Preece!' 'Just you wait, Evan Jones!' called Morgan, taking down the harp. Music rippled across the mountain top, and Evan Jones began to dance. He danced uphill and down dale. He couldn't stop.

When Bethan got back she saw Evan Jones dancing round the cottage, tottering on sore tired legs.

'Stop, Morgan! Stop!' Bethan said. 'You are playing with spite in your heart!' So Morgan stopped and Evan Jones ran off down the hill as fast as his sore tired legs could take him.

But, when Morgan looked round, the golden harp had vanished. 'Never mind,' said Bethan, 'I'll play and sing for you just as I used to.' And she did, so Morgan and Bethan and their flock of black-faced sheep were happy again and wanted for nothing.

SPEAKING AND LISTENING

Listening

- Listen to the story of 'The Magic Harp' read aloud. This is a legend, so anything can happen! Think about the *'three wizened little men in green coats'*. Who do you think they were? Where might they have come from?

- If they were fairy folk, what name might you give them (elves, pixies, goblins, gnomes)? Think of other names to describe the fairy folk.

- Evan Jones was a tenor. What does this tell you about his voice? Can you find other words for professional singers? *Baritone, soprano, bass* - these tell you how they sing. *Pop singer, opera singer, choirboy* - these tell you what they sing. Discuss the kinds of singers and songs which you like to listen to, and make a chart of your favourite songs.

Shepherds

- Morgan Preece was a shepherd. Discuss the kind of job a shepherd does. What would you like/dislike about it? The story says, *'Morgan....went out in all weathers...'* Talk about how important a good shepherd is to his flock. S/he may have to search for lost sheep in the snows of winter, carry the injured ones home, look after the sheep at lambing time. (See *Language activities*.)

- Read about the good shepherd in the Bible (John, Chapter 10). In Verse 11, Jesus says, *'I am the good shepherd: the good shepherd giveth his life for the sheep.'* Discuss why you think Jesus used this idea. What was he trying to tell the people who came to listen? Can you find more stories of shepherds in the Bible? (Look at the Christmas story.)

- Make a collection of poems about sheep and shepherds, for example, 'The Shepherd's song,' by Charles Causley, 'One shepherd' by Peter Thabit Jones. Draw, colour or paint illustrations to go with the poems. You might find pictures of shepherds and sheep on old Christmas cards. Cut out and paste into your book of poems.

Wales

- Find out where the principality of Wales is on a road map. Can you find out the name of the capital city? Morgan and Bethan *'lived in a stone cottage high in the mountains of Wales.'* Can you name a mountain in Wales? Look on the map to find out.

- Some of the place names are very long: the longest, a village in Anglesey, LLANFAIRPWLLGWYNGYLL. In full, it is Llanfairpwllgwyngyllgogerychwyrndrobwllllantysiliogogogoch, which means, *'St Mary's Church in the hollow of the white hazel near a rapid whirlpool and the Church of St Tysilio by the red cave'.* Use the letters in the name to make as many new words as you can. (See *Art activities*.)

'With spite in your heart'

- Talk about what this phrase means. Do you think Morgan was being spiteful to Evan Jones. If so, why? You have probably heard an adult say, 'Don't be spiteful!' Think about how it feels if someone is spiteful towards you. Do you think bullies *'have spite in their hearts'*? Discuss ways of dealing with bullies. (See *Language activities*.)

LANGUAGE ACTIVITIES

The Magic Harp

- Retell the story of the Magic Harp.

Your heart's desire

- Legend suggests that the three wizened little men in green coats who came to Morgan's door were from the fairy folk. *'What does your heart desire?'* they asked him. Imagine that you have been asked this question by creatures from another world.

- Write a story, in no more than a hundred words, describing a visit to your home from trolls, elves, wizards or other magic creatures. Write about what your heart would desire in terms of a skill or an ability that you don't possess, for example, being able to drive a Grand Prix car, play the saxophone, climb Everest, swim with the dolphins, and so on. Tell about your excitement/amazement when your wish is granted, and finish by describing what it is like suddenly to have a remarkable skill, like Morgan who *'ran his thick fingers over the harp strings and music rippled like mountain waters...'*

- Make a simple-fold book for your story.

On the mountain top

- Think what it would be like to live in an isolated cottage on the top of a mountain. Imagine the winds, the rain and the sunshine. What would you hear? Imagine the view you would see from the open doorway, from the window, if you looked across the roof, etc., and list these ideas in your writing notebook. Now put the ideas together to make a poem, each verse beginning with:

    Above my stone cottage......Beyond my stone cottage......Beneath my stone cottage, etc.

    Think of colours, sounds, feelings. Make it quite eerie, emphasising the isolation of the cottage.

Living on the mountain

Above my stone cottage
are clouds, fat and white,
like lost sheep straying
across the stormy sky.

Beneath my stone cottage
is/are.............................

Beyond my stone cottage
are winter winds blowing
blue and bitter, icicles
on their chilling breath.

Inside my stone cottage
is/are................................

Interviews

- Work with a partner. Choose a character from the story and plan an interview with him/her, asking how s/he felt about the strange goings-on taking place in the stone cottage on the mountain. Try to think of the character as a real person, putting yourself 'into his/her shoes'. Think about what kind of person s/he is, what they look and sound like.

- Note down questions and the most interesting answers, then jot down the interview as though it were a play. Try to begin your interviewer's questions with *why? who? what?* or *where?* You can write out the interview working together with your partner, or use the ideas to make one for yourself.

- It is a good idea to write out each part of the finished script in different-coloured inks: red for the interviewer, blue for Morgan or Bethan or Evan Jones - for someone in the village, a friend from Bethan's chapel, or one of the wizened little visitors.

Word heap

- To build a word heap from a poem or a story means selecting a required number of words from the original (10-20 is ideal) and, using as many as you can, along with others of your own choosing, making up a new poem or a short story. Try working in this way with the following selection taken from *'The Magic Harp'*, or choose some of your own.

stone	magic	sausage(s)
window(s)	door	string(s)
mountain	high	fire
angel	cake	water
table	vanished	air

Here is an example of a very short story which tries to fit in all the words. Because it is a random selection, you never quite know how the story will turn out!

Spooky story
A string of magic sausages hung from the high window, and water bubbled in the kettle on the fire. 'Angel cakes!' I said. 'I could eat a mountain of them!' She put my supper on the table and it turned to stone. She smiled and vanished into thin air. I heard the door close. I had never felt so alone.

In the poem shown in the photograph, we have tried to use all the words in the heap. It doesn't quite work, but it has the real flavour of a silly verse! Poetry isn't serious stuff all the time. You can have a lot of fun writing this kind of poem.

Letter to a bully

- In a group, discuss ways of dealing with a bully. (See *Speaking and listening.*) Try to share experiences and fears about bullying, how it feels to be challenged by a bully in the playground or on the way home.

Following the group work, write anonymous letters to a bully. He or she may be someone you know or someone you have imagined. The bully may have treated you or a friend spitefully. Use your letters to express your feelings about playground bullies.

Dear Bully,
You don't know me, but I know you. I think about you quite a lot, but I wish I didn't.
I wish you wouldn't call me names and I wish it didn't make me cry. I wish I could be the one who just walks away, and I wish I didn't care what you say. But I do.
I wish I knew why you are so spiteful. I wish I knew why you go about hitting people, and I wish I wasn't so frightened of you.
Sometimes I even wish we could be friends.   *From Anon*

Your letters might be nothing like this, but use them to say all that you have ever wished you could say to a bully. Although the bully isn't going to read them, letters will help you to deal with spite next time anyone says nasty things about you or your friend. From the ideas in the letters, make a speech bubble frieze quoting all the possible retorts that the group might want to use if/when bullying takes place.

Weathers

- Morgan, the shepherd, *'went out in all weathers...'*. Walking across the mountains in the spring sunshine would be one thing; trudging through the snow, in wind and rain, would be quite another! The poet, Thomas Hardy, wrote a famous poem called 'Weathers'. He writes about weather *'the cuckoo likes'*, then adds *'And so do I'*. In the next verse he writes about weather that the shepherd hates, then adds, *'And so do I'*.

In your notebook, jot down different weathers and think about whether shepherds would like it or hate it. Use the ideas to make your own poem, following Thomas Hardy's pattern. It might look like this:

This is the weather the shepherd likes,
and so do I,
when the sun lights up the mountain tops
and streams leap sparkling over rocks
and lambs skip through the waving grass
and so do I.

This is the weather the shepherd hates,
and so do I,
when snow covers the mountain tops
and streams are frozen and still
and sheep get lost in deep white drifts
and so do I.

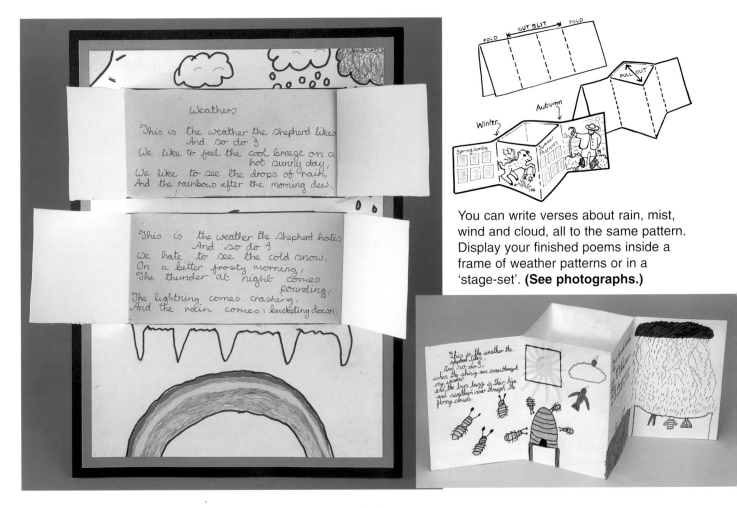

You can write verses about rain, mist, wind and cloud, all to the same pattern. Display your finished poems inside a frame of weather patterns or in a 'stage-set'. **(See photographs.)**

ART ACTIVITIES

The village with the longest name

- Draw a picture of the village of Llanfairpwllgwyngyll. (See *Speaking and listening.*) Use the image which the meaning of the name suggests in your imagination: *'St Mary's Church in the hollow of the white hazel near a rapid whirlpool and the Church of St Tysilio by the red cave'*. Use felt-tip pens to create the picture. You might like to make it into a design for a plate, a tea-towel or some other holiday souvenir with the label 'A present from Llanfairpwllgwyngyll'.

Village dancers

- When Morgan played the magic harp, *'everyone joined in the dance and the air was filled with music.'* Make a frieze showing lots of dancers leaping merrily up the mountainside, Morgan playing his harp at the top. Paint a mountain, large enough to almost fill the backing paper. Paint and cut out the figure of Morgan sitting at his harp, which can be cut from gold foil. Show Bethan dancing by his side. Then each child can paint a dancing figure in bright costume. Paste the whole scene, collage-style, to make a backdrop for a table display.

On the table, place books about Wales (recipe books, maps, places of interest, and so on). Add models or a picture of a harp, tapes with harp music and music books illustrating various stringed instruments.

The village dancers scene can be made as a tapestry collage, with each figure clothed in scraps of felt, print material, lace, and so on: the faces made from felt. Then the dancing figures are glued, collage-style as before, to the mountainside background.

Dragons

Use a large painted dragon as a focus for a writing display **(see photograph).**

For details of further Belair publications,
please write to: Libby Masters,
BELAIR PUBLICATIONS LIMITED,
Albert House, Apex Business Centre,
Boscombe Road, Dunstable, LU5 4RL.

For sales and distribution in North America and South America,
INCENTIVE PUBLICATIONS,
3835 Cleghorn Avenue, Nashville, Tn 37215.
USA.

For sales and distribution in Australia
EDUCATIONAL SUPPLIES PTY LTD
8 Cross Street, Brookvale, NSW 2100.
Australia

For sales and distribution (in other territories)
FOLENS PUBLISHERS
Albert House, Apex Business Centre,
Boscombe Road, Dunstable, LU5 4RL.
United Kingdom.
E-mail: folens@folens.com